# Sense and Sensibilia

# Sense and Sensibilia

## J. L. AUSTIN

RECONSTRUCTED FROM
THE MANUSCRIPT NOTES BY
G. J. WARNOCK

A GALAXY BOOK

New York
OXFORD UNIVERSITY PRESS
1964

© Oxford University Press 1962
First published as a Galaxy Book, 1964
Second printing, 1965
Printed in the United States of America

# FOREWORD

AUSTIN lectured many times on the problems with which this book is concerned. The first lectures which were substantially in the form here presented were those which he gave in Oxford in Trinity Term, 1947, under the general title 'Problems in Philosophy'. He first used the title 'Sense and Sensibilia' in Trinity Term of the following year, and this was the title that he subsequently retained.

In this case, as in others, Austin repeatedly revised and rewrote his own notes. Some undated and very fragmentary notes survive which are presumably those that he used in 1947. Another set of notes was prepared in 1948, and yet another in 1949. This set, in which Austin made insertions and corrections in 1955, covers the earlier parts of his argument in considerable detail; but the notes for the later lectures are much less full, and are also evidently not complete. A fourth set of notes was written in 1955, and the last in 1958, for the lectures Austin gave in the autumn of that year in the University of California. His lectures on 'Sense and Sensibilia' were given for the last time in Oxford in Hilary Term, 1959.

In addition to these more or less continuous drafts Austin's papers contained a number of separate sheets, of very various dates, on which he had made notes concerning the same range of problems. The substance of many of these was incorporated in the notes for his lectures, and therefore also in the present book. Some, however, appeared to be merely tentative and provisional; and others, though sometimes very detailed, were clearly made in the course of preparing lectures but not intended to be actually incorporated in them.

All the manuscript material is now in the Bodleian Library, and is available for study there.

The later sets of notes, those of 1955 and 1958, do not cover the topics discussed completely. They consist for the most part of additional material, and for the rest refer back, with minor rearrangements, revisions, and corrections, to the drafts of 1948 and 1949. This additional material is chiefly contained, in the present text, in section VII, the later part of section X, and in section XI. In lecturing at Berkeley Austin also used some of the material contained in his paper 'Unfair to Facts'; but this did not normally form part of his lectures on this subject, and has been omitted here since that paper itself has now appeared in print.

It is necessary to explain in some detail how the present text has been prepared. Austin certainly had it in mind that his work on perception might some day be published, but he himself had never begun to prepare it for publication. Thus his notes throughout were simply such as he needed in lecturing; and it is, from our point of view, a misfortune that he was able to lecture with complete fluency and precision without writing out his

material at all fully. Publication of his notes as they stood
was thus out of the question; in that form they would
have been unreadable, and indeed scarcely intelligible.
It was therefore decided that they should be written out
in a continuous form; and it must be carefully borne in
mind that the text which follows, while based as closely
as possible on Austin's notes, contains hardly any sentence which is a direct transcription from his own manuscript. The version here presented is at its closest to
Austin's own notes in sections I–VI, VIII, and IX, in
which his argument varied very little from 1947 onwards.
In sections VII, X, and XI, though there is no room for
serious doubt as to what Austin's argument was, it was
considerably less easy to tell from his notes exactly how,
and in what order, the argument should be deployed. In
these sections, then, the reader should be particularly
wary of attaching too much weight to every detail of the
presentation; it is here that editorial blunders are most
liable to have occurred.

Indeed, it is too much to hope that they have not crept
in elsewhere. The present text, in sheer number of words,
must have been expanded to five or six times the length
of even the most complete set of notes; and although
there is no reason to doubt that Austin's views were
substantially as they are here presented, it is impossible
to be certain that they are nowhere misrepresented in
detail. His *exact* meaning—how, for instance, he would
have expanded or qualified in lecturing some phrase, or
even some single word, appearing in his notes—was

sometimes conjectural; and at some points it is more than possible that a different editor would have favoured a different interpretation. This is doubtless inherent in the unsatisfactory, but in this case unavoidable, procedure of rewriting. The text that follows, then, cannot be read as reproducing, word for word, what Austin actually said in his lectures; nor, of course, does it come close—quite probably it comes nowhere near—to what he would have written, if he had himself prepared a text on this subject for publication. The most that can be claimed—though I venture to claim this with confidence—is that in all points of substance (and in *many* points of phraseology) his *argument* was the argument which this book contains. Indeed, if it had not been possible to make this claim, there could have been no question of publication in this form.

It should be added that the division of the text into sections is not Austin's own, and has been made merely with an eye to distinguishing the successive stages of the discussion. His own division into separate lectures was, of course, inevitably somewhat arbitrary, and also not uniform from time to time, so that it would have been neither desirable nor practicable to adhere to it.

Several of those who attended Austin's lectures, in Oxford or America, were kind enough to send me the notes they made. These were extremely helpful—particularly those of Mr. G. W. Pitcher of Princeton, and of members of the Department of Philosophy at Berkeley, which were almost as full as any of Austin's own. It is to be feared that those who heard the lectures (as I did myself in 1947) will find in this book a most imperfect approximation to what Austin said. I hope, however, that they will be willing to agree that even this kind of permanent record is better than none.

I should like to express my thanks to Mr. J. O. Urmson, who read the text in typescript and made many useful suggestions for its improvement.

G. J. WARNOCK

*November 1960*

1-14, 84-131

# CONTENTS

| I | *page* 1 | VII | *page* 62 |
|---|---|---|---|
| II | 6 | VIII | 78 |
| III | 20 | IX | 84 |
| IV | 33 | X | 104 |
| V | 44 | XI | 132 |
| VI | 55 | Index | 143 |

# I

IN THESE LECTURES I AM GOING TO DISCUSS
some current doctrines (perhaps, by now, not so
current as they once were) about sense-perception.
We shall not, I fear, get so far as to decide about
the truth or falsity of these doctrines; but in fact that is a
question that really *can't* be decided, since it turns out
that they all bite off more than they can chew. I shall take
as chief stalking-horse in the discussion Professor A. J.
Ayer's *The Foundations of Empirical Knowledge*;[1] but I
shall mention also Professor H. H. Price's *Perception*,[2]
and, later on, G. J. Warnock's book on Berkeley.[3] I find
in these texts a good deal to criticize, but I choose them
for their merits and not for their deficiencies; they seem
to me to provide the best available expositions of the
approved reasons for holding theories which are at least
as old as Heraclitus—more full, coherent, and termino-
logically exact than you find, for example, in Descartes or
Berkeley. No doubt the authors of these books no longer
hold the theories expounded in them, or at any rate
wouldn't now expound them in just the same form. But
at least they did hold them not very long ago; and of
course very numerous great philosophers have held these

[1] Macmillan, 1940.  [2] Methuen, 1932.
[3] Penguin Books, 1953.

theories, and have propounded other doctrines resulting from them. The authors I have chosen to discuss may differ from each other over certain refinements, which we shall eventually take note of—they appear to differ, for example, as to whether their central distinction is between two 'languages' or between two classes of entities—but I believe that they agree with each other, and with their predecessors, in all their major (and mostly unnoticed) assumptions.

Ideally, I suppose, a discussion of this sort ought to begin with the very earliest texts; but in this case that course is ruled out by their no longer being extant. The doctrines we shall be discussing—unlike, for example, doctrines about 'universals'—were already quite ancient in Plato's time.

The general doctrine, generally stated, goes like this: we never see or otherwise perceive (or 'sense'), or anyhow we never *directly* perceive or sense, material objects (or material things), but only sense-data (or our own ideas, impressions, sensa, sense-perceptions, percepts, &c.).

One might well want to ask how seriously this doctrine is intended, just how strictly and literally the philosophers who propound it mean their words to be taken. But I think we had better not worry about this question for the present. It is, as a matter of fact, not at all easy to answer, for, strange though the doctrine looks, we are sometimes told to take it easy—really it's just what we've all believed all along. (There's the bit where you say it and the bit where you take it back.) In any case it is clear that the doctrine is thought *worth stating*, and equally there is no doubt that people find it disturbing; so at least we can begin with the assurance that it deserves serious attention.

My general opinion about this doctrine is that it is a typically *scholastic* view, attributable, first, to an obsession with a few particular words, the uses of which are over-simplified, not really understood or carefully studied or correctly described; and second, to an obsession with a few (and nearly always the same) half-studied 'facts'. (I say 'scholastic', but I might just as well have said 'philosophical'; over-simplification, schematization, and constant obsessive repetition of the same small range of jejune 'examples' are not only not peculiar to this case, but far too common to be dismissed as an occasional weakness of philosophers.) The fact is, as I shall try to make clear, that our ordinary words are much subtler in their uses, and mark many more distinctions, than philosophers have realized; and that the facts of perception, as discovered by, for instance, psychologists but also as noted by common mortals, are much more diverse and complicated than has been allowed for. It is essential, here as elsewhere, to abandon old habits of *Gleichschaltung*, the deeply ingrained worship of tidy-looking dichotomies.

I am *not*, then—and this is a point to be clear about from the beginning—going to maintain that we ought to be 'realists', to embrace, that is, the doctrine that we *do* perceive material things (or objects). This doctrine would be no less scholastic and erroneous than its antithesis. The question, do we perceive material things or sense-data, no doubt looks very simple—*too* simple—but is entirely misleading (cp. Thales' similarly vast and over-simple question, what the world is made of). One of the most important points to grasp is that these two terms, 'sense-data' and 'material things', live by taking in each other's washing—what is spurious is not one term of the pair, but the antithesis itself.[1] There is no *one* kind of thing that we 'perceive' but many *different* kinds, the number being reducible if at all by scientific investigation and not by philosophy: pens are in many ways though not in all ways unlike rainbows, which are in many ways though not in all ways unlike after-images, which in turn are in many ways but not in all ways unlike pictures on the cinema-screen—and so on, without assignable limit. So we are *not* to look for an answer to the question, what kind of thing we perceive. What we have above all to do is, negatively, to rid ourselves of such illusions as 'the argument from illusion'—an 'argument' which those (e.g. Berkeley, Hume, Russell, Ayer) who have been most adept at working it, most fully masters of a certain special, happy style of blinkering philosophical English, have all themselves felt to be somehow spurious. There is no simple way of doing this—partly because, as we shall see, there is no simple 'argument'. It is a matter of unpicking,

[1] The case of 'universal' and 'particular', or 'individual', is similar in some respects though of course not in all. In philosophy it is often good policy, where one member of a putative pair falls under suspicion, to view the more innocent-seeming party suspiciously as well.

one by one, a mass of seductive (mainly verbal) fallacies, of exposing a wide variety of concealed motives—an operation which leaves us, in a sense, just where we began.

In a sense—but actually we may hope to learn something positive in the way of a technique for dissolving philosophical worries (*some* kinds of philosophical worry, not the whole of philosophy); and also something about the meanings of some English words ('reality', 'seems', 'looks', &c.) which, besides being philosophically very slippery, are in their own right interesting. Besides, there is nothing so plain boring as the constant repetition of assertions that are not true, and sometimes not even faintly sensible; if we can reduce this a bit, it will be all to the good.

# II

LET US HAVE A LOOK, THEN, AT THE VERY BE-
ginning of Ayer's *Foundations*—the bottom, one
might perhaps call it, of the garden path. In
these paragraphs[1] we already seem to see the
plain man, here under the implausible aspect of Ayer himself, dribbling briskly into position in front of his own
goal, and squaring up to encompass his own destruction.

It does not normally occur to us that there is any need for
us to justify our belief in the existence of material things. At
the present moment, for example, I have no doubt whatsoever that I really am perceiving the familiar objects, the
chairs and table, the pictures and books and flowers with
which my room is furnished; and I am therefore satisfied that
they exist. I recognize indeed that people are sometimes deceived by their senses, but this does not lead me to suspect
that my own sense-perceptions cannot in general be trusted,
or even that they may be deceiving me now. And this is not,
I believe, an exceptional attitude. I believe that, in practice,
most people agree with John Locke that 'the certainty of
things existing *in rerum natura*, when we have the testimony
of our senses for it, is not only as great as our frame can attain
to, but as our condition needs'.

When, however, one turns to the writings of those philosophers who have recently concerned themselves with the
subject of perception, one may begin to wonder whether this

[1] Ayer, op. cit., pp. 1–2.

matter is quite so simple. It is true that they do, in general, allow that our belief in the existence of material things is well founded; some of them, indeed, would say that there were occasions on which we knew for certain the truth of such propositions as 'this is a cigarette' or 'this is a pen'. But even so they are not, for the most part, prepared to admit that such objects as pens or cigarettes are ever directly perceived. What, in their opinion, we directly perceive is always an object of a different kind from these; one to which it is now customary to give the name of 'sense-datum'.

Now in this passage some sort of contrast is drawn between what we (or the ordinary man) believe (or believes), and what philosophers, at least 'for the most part', believe or are 'prepared to admit'. We must look at both sides of this contrast, and with particular care at what is assumed in, and implied by, what is actually said. The ordinary man's side, then, first.

1. It is clearly implied, first of all, that the ordinary man believes that he perceives material things. Now this, at least if it is taken to mean that he would *say* that he perceives material things, is surely wrong straight off; for 'material thing' is not an expression which the ordinary man would use—nor, probably, is 'perceive'. Presumably, though, the expression 'material thing' is here put forward, not as what the ordinary man would *say*, but as designating in a general way the *class* of things of which the ordinary man both believes and from time to time says that he perceives particular instances. But then we have to ask, of course, what this class comprises. We are given, as examples, 'familiar objects'—chairs, tables,

pictures, books, flowers, pens, cigarettes; the expression 'material thing' is not here (or anywhere else in Ayer's text) further defined.[1] But *does* the ordinary man believe that what he perceives is (always) something like furniture, or like these other 'familiar objects'—moderate-sized specimens of dry goods? We may think, for instance, of people, people's voices, rivers, mountains, flames, rainbows, shadows, pictures on the screen at the cinema, pictures in books or hung on walls, vapours, gases—all of which people say that they see or (in some cases) hear or smell, i.e. 'perceive'. Are these all 'material things'? If not, exactly which are not, and exactly why? No answer is vouchsafed. The trouble is that the expression 'material thing' is functioning *already*, from the very beginning, simply as a foil for 'sense-datum'; it is not here given, and is never given, any other role to play, and apart from this consideration it would surely never have occurred to anybody to try to represent as some single *kind of things* the things which the ordinary man says that he 'perceives'.

2. Further, it seems to be also implied (*a*) that when the ordinary man believes that he is not perceiving material things, he believes he is being deceived by his senses; and (*b*) that when he believes he is being deceived by his senses, he believes that he is not perceiving material things. But both of these are wrong. An ordinary man who saw, for example, a rainbow would not, if persuaded

---

[1] Compare Price's list on p. 1 of *Perception*—'chairs and tables, cats and rocks'—though he complicates matters by adding 'water' and 'the earth'. See also p. 280, on 'physical objects', 'visuo-tactual solids'.

that a rainbow is not a material thing, at once conclude that his senses were deceiving him; nor, when for instance he knows that the ship at sea on a clear day is much farther away than it looks, does he conclude that he is not seeing a material thing (still less that he *is* seeing an immaterial ship). That is to say, there is no more a simple contrast between what the ordinary man believes when all is well (that he is 'perceiving material things') and when something is amiss (that his 'senses are deceiving him' and he is *not* 'perceiving material things') than there is between what he believes that he perceives ('material things') and what philosophers for their part are prepared to admit, whatever that may be. The ground is already being prepared for *two* bogus dichotomies.

3. Next, is it not rather delicately hinted in this passage that the plain man is really a bit naïve?[1] It 'does not normally occur' to him that his belief in 'the existence of material things' needs justifying—but perhaps it *ought* to occur to him. He has 'no doubt whatsoever' that he really perceives chairs and tables—but perhaps he ought to have a doubt or two and not be so easily 'satisfied'. That people are sometimes deceived by their senses 'does not lead him to suspect' that all may not be well—but perhaps a more reflective person *would* be led to suspect. Though ostensibly the plain man's position is here just being described, a little quiet undermining is already being effected by these turns of phrase.

[1] Price, op. cit., p. 26, says that he *is* naïve, though it is not, it seems, certain that he is actually a Naïve Realist.

4. But, perhaps more importantly, it is also implied, even taken for granted, that there is *room* for doubt and suspicion, whether or not the plain man feels any. The quotation from Locke, with which most people are said to agree, in fact contains a strong *suggestio falsi*. It suggests that when, for instance, I look at a chair a few yards in front of me in broad daylight, my view is that I have (*only*) as much certainty as I need and can get that there is a chair and that I see it. But in fact the plain man would regard doubt in such a case, not as far-fetched or over-refined or somehow unpractical, but as plain *nonsense*; he would say, quite correctly, 'Well, if that's not seeing a real chair then *I don't know what is*.' Moreover, though the plain man's alleged belief that his 'sense-perceptions' can 'in general' or 'now' be trusted is implicitly contrasted with the philosophers' view, it turns out that the philosophers' view is not just that his sense-perceptions *can't* be trusted 'now', or 'in general', or as often as he thinks; for apparently philosophers 'for the most part' really maintain that what the plain man believes to be the case is really *never* the case—'what, in their opinion, we directly perceive is *always* an object of a different kind'. The philosopher is not really going to argue that things go wrong more often than the unwary plain man supposes, but that in some sense or some way he is wrong all the time. So it is misleading to hint, not only that there is always room for doubt, but that the philosophers' dissent from the plain man is just a matter of degree; it is really not *that* kind of disagreement at all.

5. Consider next what is said here about deception. We recognize, it is said, that 'people are sometimes deceived by their senses', though we think that, in general, our 'sense-perceptions' can 'be trusted'.

Now first, though the phrase 'deceived by our senses' is a common metaphor, it *is* a metaphor; and this is worth noting, for in what follows the same metaphor is frequently taken up by the expression 'veridical' and taken very seriously. In fact, of course, our senses are dumb—though Descartes and others speak of 'the testimony of the senses', our senses do not *tell* us anything, true or false. The case is made much worse here by the unexplained introduction of a quite new creation, our 'sense-perceptions'. These entities, which of course don't really figure at all in the plain man's language or among his beliefs, are brought in with the implication that whenever we 'perceive' there is an *intermediate* entity *always* present and *informing* us about something *else*— the question is, can we or can't we trust what it says? Is it 'veridical'? But of course to state the case in this way is simply to soften up the plain man's alleged views for the subsequent treatment; it is preparing the way for, by practically attributing to *him*, the so-called philosophers' view.

Next, it is important to remember that talk of deception only *makes sense* against a background of general non-deception. (You can't fool all of the people all of the time.) It must be possible to *recognize* a case of deception by checking the odd case against more normal ones. If I say, 'Our petrol-gauge sometimes deceives us', I am understood: though usually what it indicates squares with what we have in the tank, sometimes it doesn't—it sometimes points to two gallons when the tank turns out to be nearly empty. But suppose I say, 'Our crystal ball sometimes deceives us': this is puzzling, because really we haven't the least idea what the 'normal' case—*not* being deceived by our crystal ball—would actually be.

The cases, again, in which a plain man might say he was 'deceived by his senses' are not at all common. In particular, he would *not* say this when confronted with ordinary cases of perspective, with ordinary mirror-images, or with dreams; in fact, when he dreams, looks down the long straight road, or at his face in the mirror, he is not, or at least is hardly ever, *deceived* at all. This is worth remembering in view of another strong *suggestio falsi*—namely, that when the philosopher cites as cases of 'illusion' all these and many other very common phenomena, he is either simply mentioning cases which the plain man already concedes as cases of 'deception by the senses', or at any rate is only extending a bit what he would readily concede. In fact this is very far indeed from being the case.

And even so—even though the plain man certainly does not accept anything like so *many* cases as cases of being 'deceived by his senses' as philosophers seem to—it would certainly be quite wrong to suggest that he regards all the cases he *does* accept as being of just the same kind. The battle is, in fact, half lost already if this suggestion is tolerated. Sometimes the plain man would prefer to say that his senses were deceived rather than that he was deceived by his senses—the quickness of the hand deceives the eye, &c. But there is actually a great multiplicity of cases here, at least at the edges of which it is no doubt uncertain (and it would be typically scholastic to try to decide) just which are and which are not cases where the metaphor of being 'deceived by the senses' would naturally be employed. But surely even the plainest of men would want to distinguish (*a*) cases where the *sense-organ* is deranged or abnormal or in some way or other not functioning properly; (*b*) cases where the *medium*—or more generally, the conditions—of perception are in some way abnormal or off-colour; and (*c*) cases where a wrong inference is made or a wrong construction is put on things, e.g. on some sound that he hears. (Of course these cases do not exclude each other.) And then again there are the quite common cases of misreadings, mishearings, Freudian over-sights, &c., which don't seem to belong properly under any of these headings. That is to say, once again there is no neat and simple dichotomy between things going right and things going wrong; things may go wrong, as we really all know quite well, in lots of *different* ways—which don't have to be, and must not be assumed to be, classifiable in any general fashion.

Finally, to repeat here a point we've already mentioned, of course the plain man does *not* suppose that all the cases in which he is 'deceived by his senses' are alike in the particular respect that, in those cases, he is not 'perceiving material things', or *is* perceiving something not real or not material. Looking at the Müller-Lyer diagram (in which, of two lines of equal length, one looks longer than the other), or at a distant village on a very clear day across a valley, is a very different kettle of fish from seeing a ghost or from having D.T.s and seeing pink rats. And when the plain man sees on the stage the Headless Woman, what he sees (and this *is* what he sees, whether he knows it or not) is not something 'unreal' or 'immaterial', but a woman against a dark background with her head in a black bag. If the trick is well done, he doesn't (because it's deliberately made very difficult for him) properly size up what he sees, or see *what* it is; but to say this is far from concluding that he sees something *else*.

In conclusion, then, there is less than no reason to swallow the suggestions *either* that what the plain man believes that he perceives most of the time constitutes a *kind* of things (*sc.* 'material objects'), *or* that he can be said to recognize any other single *kind* of cases in which he is 'deceived'.[1] Now let us consider what it is that is said about philosophers.

Philosophers, it is said, 'are not, for the most part, prepared to admit that such objects as pens or cigarettes

---

[1] I am not denying that cases in which things go wrong *could* be lumped together under some single name. A single name might in itself be innocent enough, provided its use was not taken to imply either (*a*) that the cases were all alike, or (*b*) that they were all in certain ways alike. What matters is that the facts should not be pre-judged and (therefore) neglected.

are ever directly perceived'. Now of course what brings us up short here is the word 'directly'—a great favourite among philosophers, but actually one of the less conspicuous snakes in the linguistic grass. We have here, in fact, a typical case of a word, which already has a very special use, being gradually stretched, without caution or definition or any limit, until it becomes, first perhaps obscurely metaphorical, but ultimately meaningless. One can't abuse ordinary language without paying for it.[1]

1. First of all, it is essential to realize that here the notion of perceiving *in*directly wears the trousers— 'directly' takes whatever sense it has from the contrast with its opposite:[2] while 'indirectly' itself (*a*) has a use only in special cases, and also (*b*) has *different* uses in different cases—though that doesn't mean, of course, that there is not a good reason why we should use the same word. We might, for example, contrast the man who saw the procession directly with the man who saw it *through a periscope*; or we might contrast the place from which you can watch the door directly with the place from which you can see it only *in the mirror*. *Perhaps* we might contrast

---

[1] Especially if one abuses it without realizing what one is doing. Consider the trouble caused by unwitting stretching of the word 'sign', so as to yield—apparently—the conclusion that, when the cheese is in front of our noses, we see *signs* of cheese.

[2] Compare, in this respect, 'real', 'proper', 'free', and plenty of others. 'It's real'—what exactly are you saying it isn't? 'I wish we had a proper stair-carpet'—what are you complaining of in the one you've got? (That it's *im*proper?) 'Is he free?'—well, what have you in mind that he might be instead? In prison? Tied up in prison? Committed to a prior engagement?

seeing you directly with seeing, say, your shadow on the
blind; and *perhaps* we might contrast hearing the music
directly with hearing it relayed outside the concert-
hall. However, these last two cases suggest two further
points.

2. The first of these points is that the notion of not
perceiving 'directly' seems most at home where, as with
the periscope and the mirror, it retains its link with the
notion of a kink in *direction*. It seems that we must not be
looking *straight at* the object in question. For this reason
seeing your shadow on the blind is a doubtful case; and
seeing you, for instance, through binoculars or spectacles
is certainly not a case of seeing you *indirectly* at all. For
such cases as these last we have quite distinct contrasts
and different expressions—'with the naked eye' as opposed to 'with a telescope', 'with unaided vision' as
opposed to 'with glasses on'. (These expressions, in fact,
are much more firmly established in ordinary use than
'directly' is.)

3. And the other point is that, partly no doubt for the
above reason, the notion of indirect perception is not
naturally at home with senses other than sight. With the
other senses there is nothing quite analogous with the
'line of vision'. The most natural sense of 'hearing indirectly', of course, is that of being *told* something by an
intermediary—a quite different matter. But do I hear a
shout indirectly, when I hear the echo? If I touch you
with a barge-pole, do I touch you indirectly? Or if you
offer me a pig in a poke, might I feel the pig indirectly—

*through* the poke? And what smelling indirectly might be I have simply no idea. For this reason alone there seems to be something badly wrong with the question, 'Do we perceive things directly or not?', where perceiving is evidently intended to cover the employment of *any* of the senses.

4. But it is, of course, for other reasons too extremely doubtful how far the notion of perceiving indirectly could or should be extended. Does it, or should it, cover the telephone, for instance? Or television? Or radar? Have we moved too far in these cases from the original metaphor? They at any rate satisfy what seems to be a necessary condition—namely, concurrent existence and concomitant variation as between what is perceived in the straightforward way (the sounds in the receiver, the picture and the blips on the screen) and the candidate for what we might be prepared to describe as being perceived indirectly. And this condition fairly clearly rules out as cases of indirect perception seeing photographs (which statically record scenes from the past) and seeing films (which, though not static, are not seen contemporaneously with the events thus recorded). Certainly, there *is* a line to be drawn somewhere. It is certain, for instance, that we should not be prepared to speak of indirect perception in *every* case in which we see something from which the existence (or occurrence) of something else can be inferred; we should *not* say we see the guns indirectly, if we see in the distance only the flashes of guns.

5. Rather differently, if we are to be seriously inclined to speak of something as being perceived indirectly, it seems that it has to be the kind of thing which we (sometimes at least) just perceive, or could perceive, or which—like the backs of our own heads—others could perceive. For otherwise we don't want to say that we perceive the thing *at all*, even indirectly. No doubt there are complications here (raised, perhaps, by the electron microscope, for example, about which I know little or nothing). But it seems clear that, in general, we should want to distinguish between seeing indirectly, e.g. in a mirror, what we might have just *seen*, and seeing signs (or effects), e.g. in a Wilson cloud-chamber, of something not itself perceptible at all. It would at least not come naturally to speak of the latter as a case of perceiving something indirectly.

6. And one final point. For reasons not very obscure, we always prefer in practice what might be called the *cash-value* expression to the 'indirect' metaphor. If I were to report that I see enemy ships indirectly, I should merely provoke the question what exactly I mean. 'I mean that I can see these blips on the radar screen'—'Well, why didn't you say so then?' (Compare 'I can see an unreal duck.'—'What on earth do you mean?' 'It's a decoy duck'—'Ah, I see. Why didn't you say so at once?') That is, there is seldom if ever any particular point in actually saying 'indirectly' (or 'unreal'); the expression can cover too many rather different cases to be *just* what is wanted in any particular case.

Thus, it is quite plain that the philosophers' use of 'directly perceive', whatever it may be, is not the ordinary, or any familiar, use; for in *that* use it is not only false but simply absurd to say that such objects as pens or cigarettes are never perceived directly. But we are given no explanation or definition of this new use[1]—on the contrary, it is glibly trotted out as if we were all quite familiar with it already. It is clear, too, that the philosophers' use, whatever it may be, offends against several of the canons just mentioned above—no restrictions whatever seem to be envisaged to any special circumstances or to any of the senses in particular, and moreover it seems that what we are to be said to perceive indirectly is *never*—is not the kind of thing which ever *could* be—perceived directly.

All this lends poignancy to the question Ayer himself asks, a few lines below the passage we have been considering: 'Why may we not say that we are directly aware of material things?' The answer, he says, is provided 'by what is known as the argument from illusion'; and this is what we must next consider. Just possibly the answer may help us to understand the question.

--------

[1] Ayer takes note of this, rather belatedly, on pp. 60–61.

# III

THE PRIMARY PURPOSE OF THE ARGUMENT from illusion is to induce people to accept 'sense-data' as the proper and correct answer to the question what they perceive on certain *abnormal, exceptional* occasions; but in fact it is usually followed up with another bit of argument intended to establish that they *always* perceive sense-data. Well, what is the argument?

In Ayer's statement[1] it runs as follows. It is 'based on the fact that material things may present different appearances to different observers, or to the same observer in different conditions, and that the character of these appearances is to some extent causally determined by the state of the conditions and the observer'. As illustrations of this alleged fact Ayer proceeds to cite perspective ('a coin which looks circular from one point of view may look elliptical from another'); refraction ('a stick which normally appears straight looks bent when it is seen in water'); changes in colour-vision produced by drugs ('such as mescal'); mirror-images; double vision; hallucination; apparent variations in tastes; variations in felt warmth ('according as the hand that is feeling it is itself

[1] Ayer, op. cit., pp. 3-5.

hot or cold'); variations in felt bulk ('a coin seems larger when it is placed on the tongue than when it is held in the palm of the hand'); and the oft-cited fact that 'people who have had limbs amputated may still continue to feel pain in them'.

He then selects three of these instances for detailed treatment. First, refraction—the stick which normally 'appears straight' but 'looks bent' when seen in water. He makes the 'assumptions' (*a*) that the stick does not *really change its shape* when it is placed in water, and (*b*) that it *cannot be* both crooked and straight.[1] He then concludes ('it follows') that 'at least one of the *visual appearances* of the stick is *delusive*'. Nevertheless, even when 'what we see is not the *real quality* of a *material thing*, it is supposed that we are still seeing something'—and this something is to be called a 'sense-datum'. A sense-datum is to be 'the object of which we are *directly* aware, in perception, if it is not *part* of any *material thing*'. (The italics are mine throughout this and the next two paragraphs.)

Next, mirages. A man who sees a mirage, he says, is 'not perceiving any material thing; for the oasis which he thinks he is perceiving *does not exist*'. But 'his *experience* is not an experience of nothing'; thus 'it is said that he is experiencing sense-data, which are similar in character to what he would be experiencing if he were seeing a real oasis, but are delusive in the sense that *the*

[1] It is not only strange, but also important, that Ayer calls these 'assumptions'. Later on he is going to take seriously the notion of denying at least one of them, which he could hardly do if he had recognized them here as the plain and incontestable facts that they are.

*material thing which they appear to present* is not *really there*'.

Lastly, reflections. When I look at myself in a mirror 'my body *appears to be* some distance behind the glass'; but it cannot actually be in two places at once; thus, my perceptions in this case 'cannot all be *veridical*'. But I do see *something*; and if 'there really is no such material thing as my body in the place where it appears to be, what is it that I am seeing?' Answer—a sense-datum. Ayer adds that 'the same conclusion may be reached by taking any other of my examples'.

Now I want to call attention, first of all, to the name of this argument—the 'argument from *illusion*', and to the fact that it is produced as establishing the conclusion that some at least of our 'perceptions' are *delusive*. For in this there are two clear implications—(*a*) that all the cases cited in the argument are cases of *illusions*; and (*b*) that *illusion* and *delusion* are the same thing. But both of these implications, of course, are quite wrong; and it is by no means unimportant to point this out, for, as we shall see, the argument trades on confusion at just this point.

What, then, would be some genuine examples of illusion? (The fact is that hardly any of the cases cited by Ayer is, at any rate without stretching things, a case of illusion at all.) Well, first, there are some quite clear cases of *optical* illusion—for instance the case we mentioned earlier in which, of two lines of equal length, one is made to look longer than the other. Then again there are illusions produced by professional 'illusionists', conjurors

—for instance the Headless Woman on the stage, who is made to look headless, or the ventriloquist's dummy which is made to appear to be talking. Rather different—not (usually) produced on purpose—is the case where wheels rotating rapidly enough in one direction may look as if they were rotating quite slowly in the opposite direction. Delusions, on the other hand, are something altogether different from this. Typical cases would be delusions of persecution, delusions of grandeur. These are primarily a matter of grossly disordered beliefs (and so, probably, behaviour) and may well have nothing in particular to do with perception.[1] But I think we might also say that the patient who sees pink rats has (suffers from) delusions— particularly, no doubt, if, as would probably be the case, he is not clearly aware that his pink rats aren't real rats.[2]

The most important differences here are that the term 'an illusion' (in a perceptual context) does not suggest that something totally unreal is *conjured up*—on the contrary, there just is the arrangement of lines and arrows on the page, the woman on the stage with her head in a black bag, the rotating wheels; whereas the term 'delusion' *does* suggest something totally unreal, not really there at all. (The convictions of the man who has delusions of persecution can be *completely* without foundation.) For this reason delusions are a much more serious matter—something is really wrong, and what's more,

[1] The latter point holds, of course, for *some* uses of 'illusion' too; there are the illusions which some people (are said to) lose as they grow older and wiser.

[2] Cp. the white rabbit in the play called *Harvey*.

wrong *with* the person who has them. But when I see an optical illusion, however well it comes off, there is nothing wrong with me personally, the illusion is not a little (or a large) peculiarity or idiosyncrasy of my own; it is quite public, anyone can see it, and in many cases standard procedures can be laid down for producing it. Furthermore, if we are not actually to be taken in, we need to be *on our guard*; but it is no use to tell the sufferer from delusions to be on his guard. He needs to be cured.

Why is it that we tend—if we do—to confuse illusions with delusions? Well, partly, no doubt the terms are often used loosely. But there is also the point that people may have, without making this explicit, different views or theories about the facts of some cases. Take the case of seeing a ghost, for example. It is not generally known, or agreed, what seeing ghosts *is*. Some people think of seeing ghosts as a case of something being conjured up, perhaps by the disordered nervous system of the victim; so in their view seeing ghosts is a case of delusion. But other people have the idea that what is called seeing ghosts is a case of being taken in by shadows, perhaps, or reflections, or a trick of the light—that is, they assimilate the case in their minds to illusion. In this way, seeing ghosts, for example, may come to be labelled sometimes as 'delusion', sometimes as 'illusion'; and it may not be noticed that it makes a difference which label we use. Rather, similarly, there seem to be different doctrines in the field as to what mirages are. Some seem to take a mirage to be a vision conjured up by the crazed brain of the thirsty and exhausted traveller (delusion), while in other accounts it is a case of atmospheric refraction, whereby something below the horizon is made to appear above it (illusion). (Ayer, you may remember, takes the delusion view, although he cites it along with the rest as a case of illusion. He says not that the oasis appears to be where it is not, but roundly that 'it does not exist'.)

The way in which the 'argument from illusion' positively trades on not distinguishing illusions from delusions is, I think, this. So long as it is being suggested that the cases paraded for our attention are cases of *illusion*, there is the implication (from the ordinary use of the word) that there really is something there that we perceive. But then, when these cases begin to be quietly called delusive, there comes in the very different suggestion of something being conjured up, something unreal or at any rate 'immaterial'. These two implications taken together may then subtly insinuate that in the cases cited there really is something that we are perceiving, but that this is an immaterial something; and this insinuation, even if not conclusive by itself, is certainly well calculated to edge us a little closer towards just the position where the sense-datum theorist wants to have us.

So much, then—though certainly there could be a good deal more—about the differences between illusions and delusions and the reasons for not obscuring them. Now let us look briefly at some of the other cases Ayer lists. Reflections, for instance. No doubt you *can* produce illusions with mirrors, suitably disposed. But is just *any* case of seeing something in a mirror an illusion, as he implies? Quite obviously not. For seeing things in mirrors is a perfectly *normal* occurrence, completely familiar, and there is usually no question of anyone being taken in. No doubt, if you're an infant or an aborigine and have never come across a mirror before, you may be pretty baffled, and even visibly perturbed, when you do. But is that a reason why the rest of us should speak of illusion here? And just the same goes for the phenomena of perspective—again, one *can* play tricks with perspective, but in the ordinary case there is no question of illusion. That a round coin should 'look elliptical' (in one sense) from some points of view is exactly what we expect and what we normally find; indeed, we should be badly put out if we ever found this not to be so. Refraction again—the stick that looks bent in water—is far too familiar a case to be properly called a case of illusion. We may perhaps be prepared to agree that the stick looks bent; but then we can see that it's partly submerged in water, so that is exactly how we should expect it to look.

It is important to realize here how familiarity, so to speak, takes the edge off illusion. Is the cinema a case of illusion? Well, just possibly the first man who ever saw moving pictures may have felt inclined to say that here was a case of illusion. But in fact it's pretty unlikely that even he, even momentarily, was actually taken in; and by now the whole thing is so ordinary a part of our lives that it never occurs to us even to raise the question. One might as well ask whether producing a photograph is producing an illusion—which would plainly be just silly.

Then we must not overlook, in all this talk about illusions and delusions, that there are plenty of more or less unusual cases, not yet mentioned, which certainly aren't either. Suppose that a proof-reader makes a mistake—he fails to notice that what ought to be 'causal' is printed as 'casual'; does he have a delusion? Or is there an illusion before him? Neither, of course; he simply *misreads*. Seeing after-images, too, though not a particularly frequent occurrence and not just an ordinary case of seeing, is neither seeing illusions nor having delusions. And what about dreams? Does the dreamer see illusions? Does he have delusions? Neither; dreams are *dreams*.

Let us turn for a moment to what Price has to say about illusions. He produces,[1] by way of saying 'what the term "illusion" means', the following 'provisional definition': 'An illusory sense-datum of sight or touch is a sense-datum which is such that we tend to take it to be part of the surface of a material object, but if we take it so we are wrong.' It is by no means clear, of course, what this dictum itself means; but still, it seems fairly clear that the definition doesn't actually fit all the cases of illusion. Consider the two lines again. Is there anything here which we tend to take, wrongly, to be part of the surface of a material object? It doesn't seem so. We just see the two lines, we don't think or even tend to think that we

[1] *Perception*, p. 27.

see anything else, we aren't even raising the question whether anything is or isn't 'part of the surface' of—what, anyway? the lines? the page?—the trouble is just that one line looks longer than the other, though it isn't. Nor surely, in the case of the Headless Woman, is it a question whether anything is or isn't part of her surface; the trouble is just that she looks as if she had no head.

It is noteworthy, of course, that, before he even begins to consider the 'argument from illusion', Price has already incorporated in this 'definition' the idea that in such cases there is something to be seen *in addition to* the ordinary things—which is part of what the argument is commonly used, and not uncommonly taken, to *prove*. But this idea surely has no place in an attempt to say what 'illusion' *means*. It comes in again, improperly I think, in his account of perspective (which incidentally he also cites as a species of illusion)—'a distant hillside which is full of protuberances, and slopes upwards at quite a gentle angle, will appear flat and vertical. . . . This means that the sense-datum, the colour-expanse which we sense, actually *is* flat and vertical.' But why should we accept this account of the matter? Why should we say that there is *anything* we see which *is* flat and vertical, though not 'part of the surface' of any material object? To speak thus is to assimilate all such cases to cases of delusion, where there *is* something not 'part of any material thing'. But we have already discussed the undesirability of this assimilation.

Next, let us have a look at the account Ayer himself

gives of some at least of the cases he cites. (In fairness we must remember here that Ayer has a number of quite substantial reservations of his own about the merits and efficacy of the argument from illusion, so that it is not easy to tell just how seriously he intends his exposition of it to be taken; but this is a point we shall come back to.)

First, then, the familiar case of the stick in water. Of this case Ayer says (*a*) that since the stick looks bent but is straight, 'at least one of the visual appearances of the stick is *delusive*'; and (*b*) that 'what we see [directly anyway] is not the real quality of [a few lines later, not part of] a material thing'. Well now: does the stick 'look bent' to begin with? I think we can agree that it does, we have no better way of describing it. But of course it does *not* look *exactly* like a bent stick, a bent stick out of water—at most, it may be said to look rather like a bent stick partly immersed *in* water. After all, we can't help seeing the water the stick is partly immersed in. So exactly what in this case is supposed to be *delusive*? What is wrong, what is even faintly surprising, in the idea of a stick's being straight but looking bent sometimes? Does anyone suppose that if something is straight, then it jolly well has to *look* straight at all times and in all circumstances? Obviously no one seriously supposes this. So what mess are we supposed to get into here, what is the difficulty? For of course it has to be suggested that there *is* a difficulty—a difficulty, furthermore, which calls for a pretty radical solution, the introduction of sense-data. But what is the problem we are invited to solve in this way?

Well, we are told, in this case you are seeing *something*; and what is this something 'if it is not part of any material thing'? But this question is, really, completely mad. The straight part of the stick, the bit not under water, is presumably part of a material thing; don't we see that? And what about the bit *under* water?—we can see that too. We can see, come to that, the water itself. In fact what we see is *a stick partly immersed in water*; and it is particularly extraordinary that this should appear to be called in question—that a question should be raised about *what* we are seeing—since this, after all, is simply the description of the situation with which we started. It was, that is to say, agreed at the start that we were looking at a stick, a 'material thing', part of which was under water. If, to take a rather different case, a church were cunningly camouflaged so that it looked like a barn, how could any serious question be raised about what we see when we look at it? We see, of course, *a church* that now *looks like a barn*. We do *not* see an immaterial barn, an immaterial church, or an immaterial anything else. And what in this case could seriously tempt us to say that we do?

Notice, incidentally, that in Ayer's description of the stick-in-water case, which is supposed to be prior to the drawing of any philosophical conclusions, there has already crept in the unheralded but important expression 'visual appearances'—it is, of course, ultimately to be suggested that all we *ever* get when we see is a visual appearance (whatever that may be).

Consider next the case of my reflection in a mirror.

My body, Ayer says, 'appears to be some distance behind the glass'; but as it's in front, it can't really be behind the glass. So what am I seeing? A sense-datum. What about this? Well, once again, although there is no objection to saying that my body 'appears to be some distance behind the glass', in saying this we must remember what sort of situation we are dealing with. It does not 'appear to be' there in a way which might tempt me (though it might tempt a baby or a savage) to go round the back and look for it, and be astonished when this enterprise proved a failure. (To say that A is *in* B doesn't always mean that if you open B you will find A, just as to say that A is *on* B doesn't always mean that you could pick it off—consider 'I saw my face in the mirror', 'There's a pain in my toe', 'I heard him on the radio', 'I saw the image on the screen', &c. Seeing something in a mirror is not like seeing a bun in a shop-window.) But does it follow that, since my body is not actually located behind the mirror, I am not seeing a material thing? Plainly not. For one thing, I can see the mirror (nearly always anyway). I can see my own body 'indirectly', *sc.* in the mirror. I can also see the re- flection of my own body or, as some would say, a mirror- image. And a mirror-image (if we choose this answer) is not a 'sense-datum'; it can be photographed, seen by any number of people, and so on. (Of course there is no question here of either illusion or delusion.) And if the question is pressed, what actually *is* some distance, five feet say, behind the mirror, the answer is, not a sense- datum, but some region of the adjoining room.

The mirage case—at least if we take the view, as Ayer does, that the oasis the traveller thinks he can see 'does not exist'—is significantly more amenable to the treatment it is given. For here we are supposing the man to be genuinely deluded, he is *not* 'seeing a material thing'.[1] We don't actually have to say, however, even here that he is 'experiencing sense-data'; for though, as Ayer says above, 'it is convenient to give a name' to what he is experiencing, the fact is that it already has a name—a *mirage*. Again, we should be wise not to accept too readily the statement that what he is experiencing is '*similar in character* to what he would be experiencing if he were seeing a real oasis'. For is it at all likely, really, to be very similar? And, looking ahead, if we were to concede this point we should find the concession being used against us at a later stage—namely, at the stage where we shall be invited to agree that we see sense-data always, in normal cases too.

[1] Not even 'indirectly', no such thing is 'presented'. Doesn't this seem to make the case, though more amenable, a good deal less useful to the philosopher? It's hard to see how normal cases could be said to be *very like* this.

# IV

IN DUE COURSE WE SHALL HAVE TO CONSIDER
Ayer's own 'evaluation' of the argument from illusion, what in his opinion it establishes and why.
But for the present I should like to direct attention
to another feature of his exposition of the argument—a
feature which in fact seems to be common to the expositions of most philosophers. In the course of setting out
the cases on which the argument is based, Ayer makes
pretty free use of the expressions 'look', 'appear', and
'seem'—apparently, in the manner of most other philosophers, attaching no great importance to the question
which expression is used where, and indeed implying by
the speed of his philosophical flight that they could be
used interchangeably, that there is nothing much to
choose between them. But this is not so; the expressions
in question actually have *quite* different uses, and it often
makes a *great* difference which one you use. Not always,
certainly—there are cases, as we shall see, in which they
come down to much the same, contexts in which they
really are more or less interchangeable. But it would be
just a mistake to conclude that, because there are such
cases, there isn't *any* particular difference in the uses of
the words; there is, and there are plenty of contexts and
constructions which show this.[1] The only thing to do

[1] Compare the expressions 'right', 'ought', 'duty', 'obligation'—here

here, by way of avoiding misguided assimilations, is to consider numerous examples of uses of these expressions, until in the end we get the feel of the thing.

First, then, 'looks'. Here we have at least the following kinds of cases and constructions:

1. (*a*)  It looks blue (round, angular, &c.).
   (*b*)  He looks a gentleman (a tramp, a sport, a typical Englishman).
   She looks *chic* (a fright, a regular frump).

Here we have the verb directly followed by an adjective or adjectival phrase.

2. (*a*)  It [a colour] looks like blue [the colour].
   It looks like a recorder.
   (*b*)  He looks like a gentleman (a sailor, a horse).

Here we have 'looks like' (cp. 'sounds like') followed by a noun.

3. (*a*)  It looks as if $\begin{Bmatrix} \text{it is} \\ \text{it were} \end{Bmatrix}$ raining (empty, hollow).

   (*b*)  He looks as if $\begin{Bmatrix} \text{he is} \\ \text{he were} \end{Bmatrix}$ 60 (going to faint).

4. (*a*)  It looks as though we shan't be able to get in.
   (*b*)  He looks as though he's worried about something.

too, there are contexts in which *any* of these words could be used, but large and important differences all the same in the uses of each. And here too these differences have been generally neglected by philosophers.

Now let's try 'appears':

1. (*a*)  It appears blue (upside down, elongated, &c.).
   (*b*)  He appears a gentleman.
2. (*a*)  It appears like blue.
   (*b*)  He appears like a gentleman.

(It is very doubtful, though, whether this construction with 'appears' is really defensible; it certainly rings very dubiously to my ear.)

3 (and 4). (*a*)  It appears as if (as though) . . .
   (*b*)  He appears as if (as though) . . .
5. (*a*)  It appears to expand.
   It appears to be a forgery.
   (*b*)  He appears to like her (to have recovered his temper).
   He appears to be an Egyptian.
6. (*a*)  It appears as a dark speck on the horizon.
   (*b*)  He appears as a man of good character (*sc.* from this narrative. We can also say of an actor that he 'appeared as Napoleon'.)
7.     It appears that they've all been eaten.

Notice particularly that here we have constructions (viz. 5–7) which do *not* occur with 'looks'.[1] These are in some ways the most important cases to attend to.

[1] Perhaps some of them do occur, in colloquial speech. Well, if they do, they do. But colloquial speech is often a bit *loose*, and we know—or some of us do—when this is so. We don't, of course, if we don't know the language very well, or if we're anyway rather insensitive about such matters.

Of 'seems' we can say briefly that it shares the constructions of 'appears'—though with fewer doubts about the propriety of (2). ('It seems like old times', 'It all seems like a nightmare')—*except* that 'seems' shows no construction analogous with (6), an important divergence.

Now how are we to tell the differences between these different words in these different constructions? Well, one difference certainly leaps to the eye: 'looks' is, to put it very roughly, restricted to the general sphere of *vision*, whereas the use of 'appears' or 'seems' does *not* require, or imply, the employment of any one of the senses in particular.[1] Thus, there is also a number of words analogous with 'looks', viz. 'sounds', 'smells', 'tastes', 'feels', each of which does for its own particular sense (nearly enough) just what 'looks' does for the sense of sight.

But we must look, of course, for the minuter differences; and here we must look again at some more examples, asking ourselves in just what circumstances we would say which, and why.

Consider, then: (1) He looks guilty.
          (2) He appears guilty.
          (3) He seems guilty.

We would say the first of these things simply by way of commenting on his *looks*—he has the look of a guilty

---

[1] No doubt we often enough use 'looks' where we don't mean, simply or literally, 'looks to the eye'; naturally enough, though, for we stretch the use of 'see' in just the same way.

man.[1] The second, I suggest, would typically be used with reference to certain *special circumstances*—'I quite agree that, when he's prevaricating over all those searching questions about what he did with the money, he appears guilty, but most of the time his demeanour [not just 'his looks'] is innocence itself.' And the third, fairly clearly, makes an implicit reference to certain *evidence*—evidence bearing, of course, on the question whether he *is* guilty, though not such as to settle that question conclusively— 'On the evidence we've heard so far, he certainly seems guilty.'

Consider too: (1) 'The hill looks steep'—it has the look of a steep hill; (2) 'The hill appears steep'—when you look at it from down here; (3) 'The hill seems steep'—to judge by the fact that we've had to change gear twice. Also

(1) 'She looks *chic*'—straightforward enough;

(2) 'She seems (to be) *chic*'— from these photographs, from what they've told me about her, &c.;

(3) 'She appears (to be) *chic*'—(there is, in fact, something pretty dubious about this locution, but *perhaps* she 'appears to be *chic*' in unsophisticated, provincial circles).

Plainly enough, then, even without going into much detail, the root ideas behind the uses of 'looks', 'appears', and 'seems' are not the same; and very often, where we

[1] Note the difference between 'not liking his looks' and 'not liking his appearance'; and note that we may wish to 'keep up appearances' for many different reasons, *one* of which might be just 'for the look of the thing'.

could use one word we couldn't use another. A man who seems to be guilty may quite well not *look* guilty. However, it is easy enough to see that in suitable contexts they may come very close together: for example, that somebody looks ill may *be* the evidence on which we could also remark that he seems to be ill; or again our comment on the way something looks may *be* a comment on the way it appears when viewed in particular circumstances. But naturally this will not be so *either* when the way something looks is wholly inadequate evidence (it would be rash to say that her jewellery seems to be genuine just because it looks genuine); *or* when the way something looks is wholly conclusive (what more must she do to *be* chic than to *look chic*?); *or*, for that matter, when something's really being such-and-such is not in question at all ('He looks like his father'—but no one is going to say that he seems to *be* his father). Then again, there are certain special cases in which how something looks (feels, &c.) is either all we can get to know about it in the nature of the case, or all that we normally have any interest in; we don't normally bother to make any distinction between 'The sun feels hot' and 'The sun is hot', 'The sky is blue' and 'The sky looks blue'.

That we say 'seems' when, in general, we have some but not conclusive evidence carries with it that 'seems' is compatible with 'may be' and 'may not be': 'He may be guilty; he certainly seems guilty', 'He certainly seems to be guilty, but he may not be'. 'Seems' *may* also occur in conjunction with 'is' or 'is not'; but this will usually be found to involve a shift in the evidence implicitly referred to. If I were to say, 'He certainly seems to be guilty, but he isn't', I would not usually mean that the *very same evidence* on which he seems to be guilty establishes that he is not, but that while, say, on the evidence presented *so far* (or publicly available) he seems to be guilty, there is (or I have) *further* evidence which shows that he is not. Of course I *might* assert or deny his guilt in the teeth of all the evidence there is; but this is not, and could not be, the normal case.

The construction 'seems like', however, calls for special treatment. Its function seems to be that of conveying the *general impression* which something makes; and though this sometimes comes close to 'seems to be' ('It seemed $\begin{Bmatrix} \text{like} \\ \text{to be} \end{Bmatrix}$ a serious inquiry'), often it does not. The general impression, that is, *may* be taken as evidence; but often, it will not be. 'The next three days seemed like one long nightmare' does not mean that they really seemed *to be*, that I was inclined to think they *were*, an actual nightmare. If anything, it means that that is what they *were* like—in such a context there is little to choose between 'seems' and 'is'.

There is, of course, no *general* answer at all to the question how 'looks' or 'looks like' is related to 'is'; it depends on the full circumstances of particular cases. Clearly, if I say that petrol looks like water, I am simply commenting on the way petrol looks; I am under no temptation to think, nor do I imply, that perhaps petrol *is* water. Similarly with 'A recorder sounds like a flute'. But 'This looks like water' ('That sounds like a flute') may be a different matter; if I don't already know what 'this' is, then I *may* be taking the fact that it looks like water as a ground for thinking it *is* water. But also I may not be. In saying, 'That sounds like a flute' all I am *saying* is that the sound is of a certain character; this may or may not be, and may or may not be intended and taken as, evidence of what the instrument is, what is making the sound. How it *is* intended and taken will depend on further facts about the occasion of utterance; the words themselves imply nothing either way.

Then there are differences of another kind in the ways in which 'looks like' may be meant and may be taken. We are about to watch, from seats high up at the back of the stadium, a football match in which one of the teams is Japanese. One of the teams comes running into the arena. I might say,

(1) 'They look like ants'; or
(2) 'They look like Europeans'.

Now it is plain enough that, in saying (1), I do *not* mean either that I am inclined to think some ants have come on to the field, or that the players, on inspection, would be found to look exactly, or even rather, like ants. (I may know quite well, and even be able to see, that for instance they haven't got that very striking sort of nipped-in waist.) I mean, of course, that people seen from this vast distance look (rather) like ants seen from the sort of distance at which one normally sees ants—say about six feet. Whereas, in saying (2), I *may* mean that the team now taking the field is composed of Europeans, or at least that going by their looks I think so; or I may mean that (though I know this team to be the Japanese one) the players, to my surprise perhaps, look like Europeans, are like Europeans to look at. Compare 'The moon looks no bigger than a sixpence'—it doesn't look as if it *is* no bigger than a sixpence, or as a sixpence would look if it were as far away as the moon; it looks, of course, somewhat as a sixpence looks if you look at it at about arm's length.

Some of these complications are attributable to, or at least are also found with, the word 'like' itself, and not specially with 'looks like'. Consider, 'That cloud is like a horse' and 'That animal is like a horse'. In the case of the cloud, even if we had said it was *exactly* like a horse, we should not have meant that one might easily mistake it for a horse, succumb to the temptation to try to ride it, &c. But if an *animal* is said to be like a horse, then probably it might in some circumstances be mistaken for a horse, someone might think of trying to ride it, &c.[1] Here too, then, it is not enough simply to examine the words themselves; just what is meant and what can be inferred (if anything) can be decided only by examining the full circumstances in which the words are used. We

[1] Note that, contrary to what some philosophical theories seem to imply, the notion of *being* a so-and-so must be prior to that of being *like* a so-and-so. 'Well may the animal be called a pig for it certainly eats like one'—how many things are wrong with that remark?

have already mentioned the point that, when we say of the stick partly immersed in water that it 'looks bent', it has to be remembered what sort of situation we are dealing with; it certainly can't be assumed that, when we use that expression in that situation, we mean that the stick really looks exactly like, might well be mistaken for, a stick that was actually bent. And we might add here that descriptions of dreams, for example, plainly can't be taken to have exactly the same force and implications as the same words would have, if used in the description of ordinary waking experiences. In fact, it is just because we all know that dreams are *throughout un*like waking experiences that we can safely use ordinary expressions in the narration of them; the peculiarity of the dream-context is sufficiently well known for nobody to be misled by the fact that we speak in ordinary terms.

Two final points. First, it is worth emphasizing, in view of what many philosophers have said, that descriptions of looks are neither 'incorrigible' nor 'subjective'. Of course, with very familiar words such as 'red', it is no doubt pretty unlikely that we should make mistakes (though what about marginal cases?). But certainly someone might say, 'It looks heliotrope', and then have doubts *either* as to whether 'heliotrope' is right for the colour this thing looks, *or* (taking another look) as to whether this thing really looks heliotrope. There is certainly nothing *in principle* final, conclusive, irrefutable about anyone's statement that so-and-so looks such-and-such. And even if I say, ' . . . looks . . . *to me now*', I may, on being pressed, or after looking at the thing more attentively, wish to retract my statement or at least amend it. To rule out other people and other times is not to rule out uncertainty altogether, or *every* possibility of being challenged and perhaps proved wrong. It is perhaps even clearer that the way things look is, in general, just as much a fact about the world, just as open to public confirmation or challenge, as the way things are. I am not disclosing a fact about *myself*, but about petrol, when I say that petrol looks like water.

Lastly, a point about 'seems'. It is significant that we can preface a judgement or expression of opinion by the phrases 'To judge from its looks . . .' or 'Going by appearances . . .'; but we can't say, 'To judge by the *seemings* . . .'—no such substantive exists. Why not? Is it not that, whereas looks and appearances provide us with *facts* on which a judgement may be based, to speak of how things seem is *already* to express a judgement? This is, in fact, highly indicative of the special, peculiar function of 'seems'.

# V

I WANT NOW TO TAKE UP AGAIN THE PHILO-
sophical argument as it is set out in the texts we
are discussing. As I mentioned earlier, the argument from illusion is intended primarily to persuade
us that, in certain exceptional, abnormal situations, what
we perceive—directly anyway—is a sense-datum; but
then there comes a second stage, in which we are to be
brought to agree that what we (directly) perceive is *always* a sense-datum, even in the normal, unexceptional
case. It is this second stage of the argument that we must
now examine.

Ayer expounds the argument thus.[1] There is, he
says, 'no intrinsic difference in kind between those of our
perceptions that are veridical in their presentation of
material things and those that are delusive. When I look at
a straight stick, which is refracted in water and so appears
crooked, my experience is qualitatively the same as if I
were looking at a stick that really was crooked. . . .' If,
however, 'when our perceptions were delusive, we were
always perceiving something of a different kind from
what we perceived when they were veridical, we should
expect our experience to be qualitatively different in the
two cases. We should expect to be able to tell from the

[1] Ayer, op. cit., pp. 5–9.

intrinsic character of a perception whether it was a perception of a sense-datum or of a material thing. But this is not possible. . . .' Price's exposition of this point,[1] to which Ayer refers us, is in fact not perfectly analogous; for Price has already somehow reached the conclusion that we are always aware of sense-data, and here is trying to establish only that we cannot distinguish *normal* sense-data, as 'parts of the surfaces of material things', from *abnormal* ones, not 'parts of the surfaces of material things'. However, the argument used is much the same: 'the abnormal crooked sense-datum of a straight stick standing in water is qualitatively indistinguishable from a normal sense-datum of a crooked stick'; but 'is it not incredible that two entities so similar in all these qualities should really be so utterly different: that the one should be a real constituent of a material object, wholly independent of the observer's mind and organism, while the other is merely the fleeting product of his cerebral processes?'

It is argued further, both by Ayer and Price, that 'even in the case of veridical perceptions we are not directly aware of material things' [or *apud* Price, that our sense-data are not parts of the surfaces of material things] for the reason that 'veridical and delusive perceptions may form a continuous series. Thus, if I gradually approach an object from a distance I may begin by having a series of perceptions which are delusive in the sense that the object appears to be smaller than it really is. Let us

[1] *Perception*, p. 31.

assume that this series terminates in a veridical perception.[1] Then the difference in quality between this perception and its immediate predecessor will be of the same order as the difference between any two delusive perceptions that are next to one another in the series. . . .' But 'these are differences of degree and not of kind. But this, it is argued, is not what we should expect if the veridical perception were a perception of an object of a different sort, a material thing as opposed to a sense-datum. Does not the fact that veridical and delusive perceptions shade into one another in the way that is indicated by these examples show that the objects that are perceived in either case are generically the same? And from this it would follow, if it was acknowledged that the delusive perceptions were perceptions of sense-data, that what we directly experienced was always a sense-datum and never a material thing.' As Price puts it, 'it seems most extraordinary that there should be a total difference of nature where there is only an infinitesimal difference of quality'.[2]

Well, what are we to make of the arguments thus set before us?

1. It is pretty obvious, for a start, that the terms in

[1] But what, we may ask, does this assumption amount to? From what distance *does* an object, a cricket-ball say, 'look the size that it really is'? Six feet? Twenty feet?

[2] I omit from consideration a further argument cited by both Price and Ayer, which makes play with the 'causal dependence' of our 'perceptions' upon the conditions of observation and our own 'physiological and psychological states'.

which the argument is stated by Ayer are grossly ten-
dentious. Price, you remember, is not producing the
argument as a proof that we are always aware of sense-
data; in his view that question has already been settled,
and he conceives himself to be faced here only with the
question whether any sense-data are 'parts of the surfaces
of material objects'. But in Ayer's exposition the argument *is* put forward as a ground for the conclusion that
what we are (directly) aware of in perception is always a
sense-datum; and if so, it seems a rather serious defect
that this conclusion is practically assumed from the very
first sentence of the statement of the argument itself. In
that sentence Ayer uses, not indeed for the first time, the
term 'perceptions' (which incidentally has never been defined or explained), and takes it for granted, here and
throughout, that there is at any rate some kind of entities
of which we are aware in absolutely all cases—namely,
'perceptions', delusive or veridical. But of course, if one
has already been induced to swallow the idea that every
case, whether 'delusive' or 'veridical', supplies us with 'perceptions', one is only too easily going to be made to feel
that it would be straining at a gnat not to swallow sense-
data in an equally comprehensive style. But in fact one has
not even been told what 'perceptions' *are*; and the assumption of their ubiquity has been slipped in without any
explanation or argument whatever. But if those to whom
the argument is ostensibly addressed were not thus made
to concede the essential point from the beginning, would
the statement of the argument be quite such plain sailing?

2. Of course we shall also want to enter a protest against the argument's bland assumption of a simple dichotomy between 'veridical and delusive experiences'. There is, as we have already seen, *no* justification at all *either* for lumping all so-called 'delusive' experiences together, *or* for lumping together all so-called 'veridical' experiences. But again, could the argument run quite so smoothly without this assumption? It would certainly—and this, incidentally, would be all to the good—take rather longer to state.

3. But now let us look at what the argument actually says. It begins, you will remember, with an alleged statement of fact—namely, that 'there is no intrinsic difference in kind between those of our perceptions that are veridical in their presentation of material things and those that are delusive' (Ayer), that 'there is no qualitative difference between normal sense-data as such and abnormal sense-data as such' (Price). Now, waiving so far as possible the numerous obscurities in and objections to this manner of speaking, let us ask whether what is being alleged here is actually true. Is it the case that 'delusive and veridical experiences' are not 'qualitatively different'? Well, at least it seems perfectly extraordinary to say so in this sweeping way. Consider a few examples. I may have the experience (dubbed 'delusive' presumably) of dreaming that I am being presented to the Pope. Could it be seriously suggested that having this dream is 'qualitatively indistinguishable' from *actually being* presented to the Pope? Quite obviously not. After all, we have the phrase

'a dream-like quality'; some waking experiences are said to have this dream-like quality, and some artists and writers occasionally try to impart it, usually with scant success, to their works. But of course, if the fact here alleged *were* a fact, the phrase would be perfectly meaningless, because applicable to everything. If dreams were not 'qualitatively' different from waking experiences, then *every* waking experience would be like a dream; the dream-like quality would be, not difficult to capture, but impossible to avoid.[1] It is true, to repeat, that dreams are *narrated* in the same terms as waking experiences: these terms, after all, are the best terms we have; but it would be wildly wrong to conclude from this that what is narrated in the two cases is *exactly alike*. When we are hit on the head we sometimes say that we 'see stars'; but for all that, seeing stars when you are hit on the head is *not* 'qualitatively' indistinguishable from seeing stars when you look at the sky.

Again, it is simply not true to say that seeing a bright green after-image against a white wall is exactly like seeing a bright green patch actually on the wall; or that seeing a white wall through blue spectacles is exactly like seeing a blue wall; or that seeing pink rats in D.T.s is exactly like really seeing pink rats; or (once again) that seeing a stick refracted in water is exactly like seeing a bent stick. In all these cases we may *say* the same things ('It looks blue', 'It looks bent', &c.), but this is no reason

[1] This is part, no doubt *only* part, of the absurdity in Descartes' toying with the notion that the whole of our experience might be a dream.

at all for denying the obvious fact that the 'experiences'
are *different*.

4. Next, one may well wish at least to ask for the cre-
dentials of a curious general principle on which both
Ayer and Price seem to rely,[1] to the effect that, if two
things are not 'generically the same', the same 'in nature',
then they can't be alike, or even very nearly alike. If it
were true, Ayer says, that from time to time we perceived
things of two different kinds, then 'we should expect'
them to be qualitatively different. But why on earth
should we?—particularly if, as he suggests would be the
case, we never actually found such a thing to be true. It
is not at all easy to discuss this point sensibly, because of
the initial absurdity in the hypothesis that we perceive
just *two* kinds of things. But if, for example, I had never
seen a mirror, but were told (*a*) that in mirrors one sees
reflections of things, and (*b*) that reflections of things are
not 'generically the same' as things, is there any reason
why I should forthwith *expect* there to be some whacking
big 'qualitative' difference between seeing things and
seeing their reflections? Plainly not; if I were prudent, I
should simply wait and see what seeing reflections was
like. If I am told that a lemon is generically different from
a piece of soap, do I 'expect' that no piece of soap could
look just like a lemon? Why should I?

(It is worth noting that Price helps the argument along
at this point by a bold stroke of rhetoric: how *could* two
entities be 'qualitatively indistinguishable', he asks, if

---

[1] Ayer in fact expresses qualms later: see p. 12.

one is a 'real constituent of a material object', the other *'a fleeting product of his cerebral processes'*? But how in fact are we supposed to have been persuaded that sense-data are *ever* fleeting products of cerebral processes? Does this colourful description fit, for instance, the reflection of my face in a mirror?)

5. Another erroneous principle which the argument here seems to rely on is this: that it *must* be the case that 'delusive and veridical experiences' are not (as such) 'qualitatively' or 'intrinsically' distinguishable—for if they were distinguishable, we should never be 'deluded'. But of course this is not so. From the fact that I am sometimes 'deluded', mistaken, taken in through failing to distinguish A from B, it does not follow at all that A and B must be *indistinguishable*. Perhaps I should have noticed the difference if I had been more careful or attentive; perhaps I am just bad at distinguishing things of this sort (e.g. vintages); perhaps, again, I have never learned to discriminate between them, or haven't had much practice at it. As Ayer observes, probably truly, 'a child who had not learned that refraction was a means of distortion would naturally believe that the stick really was crooked as he saw it'; but how is the fact that an uninstructed child probably would not discriminate between *being refracted* and *being crooked* supposed to establish the allegation that there *is* no 'qualitative' difference between the two cases? What sort of reception would I be likely to get from a professional tea-taster, if I were to say to him, 'But there can't be any difference between the flavours of these two

brands of tea, for I regularly fail to distinguish between them'? Again, when 'the quickness of the hand deceives the eye', it is not that what the hand is really doing is *exactly like* what we are tricked into thinking it is doing, but simply that it is *impossible to tell* what it is really doing. In this case it may be true that we can't distinguish, and not merely that we don't; but even this doesn't mean that the two cases are exactly alike.

I do not, of course, wish to deny that there may be cases in which 'delusive and veridical experiences' really are 'qualitatively indistinguishable'; but I certainly do wish to deny (*a*) that such cases are anything like as *common* as both Ayer and Price seem to suppose, and (*b*) that there *have* to be such cases to accommodate the undoubted fact that we are sometimes 'deceived by our senses'. We are not, after all, quasi-infallible beings, who can be taken in only where the avoidance of mistake is completely impossible. But if we are prepared to admit that there may be, even that there are, *some* cases in which 'delusive and veridical perceptions' really are indistinguishable, does this admission require us to drag in, or even to let in, sense-data? No. For even if we were to make the prior admission (which we have so far found no reason to make) that in the 'abnormal' cases we perceive sense-data, we should not be obliged to extend this admission to the 'normal' cases too. For why on earth should it *not* be the case that, in some few instances, perceiving one sort of thing is exactly like perceiving another?

6. There is a further quite general difficulty in assessing

the force of this argument, which we (in common with the authors of our texts) have slurred over so far. The question which Ayer invites us to consider is whether two classes of 'perceptions', the veridical and the delusive, are or are not 'qualitatively different', 'intrinsically different in kind'; but how are we supposed to set about even considering this question, when we are not told what 'a perception' *is*? In particular, how many of the circumstances of a situation, as these would ordinarily be stated, are supposed to be included in 'the perception'? For example, to take the stick in water again: it is a feature of this case that part of the stick is under water, and water, of course, is not invisible; is the water, then, part of 'the perception'? It is difficult to conceive of any grounds for denying that it is; but *if* it is, surely this is a perfectly obvious respect in which 'the perception' differs from, is distinguishable from, the 'perception' we have when we look at a bent stick *not* in water. There is a sense, perhaps, in which the presence or absence of water is not the *main thing* in this case—we are supposed to be addressing ourselves primarily to questions about the stick. But in fact, as a great quantity of psychological investigation has shown, discrimination between one thing and another very frequently depends on such more or less extraneous concomitants of the main thing, even when such concomitants are not consciously taken note of. As I said, we are told nothing of what 'a perception' is; but could any defensible account, if such an account were offered, completely exclude all these highly significant attendant circumstances? And if they *were* excluded—in some more or less arbitrary way—how much interest or importance would be left in the contention that 'delusive' and 'veridical' perceptions are indistinguishable? Inevitably, if you rule out the respects in which A and B differ, you may expect to be left with respects in which they are alike.

I conclude, then, that this part of the philosophical argument involves (though not in every case equally essentially) (*a*) acceptance of a quite bogus dichotomy of all 'perceptions' into two groups, the 'delusive' and the 'veridical'—to say nothing of the unexplained introduction of 'perceptions' themselves; (*b*) an implicit but grotesque exaggeration of the *frequency* of 'delusive perceptions'; (*c*) a further grotesque exaggeration of the *similarity* between 'delusive' perceptions and 'veridical' ones; (*d*) the erroneous suggestion that there *must* be such similarity, or even qualitative *identity*; (*e*) the acceptance of the pretty gratuitous idea that things 'generically different' could not be qualitatively alike; and (*f*)—which is really a corollary of (*c*) and (*a*)—the gratuitous neglect of those more or less subsidiary features which often make possible the discrimination of situations which, in other *broad* respects, may be roughly alike. These seem to be rather serious deficiencies.

# VI

AYER, OF COURSE, DOES NOT HIMSELF ACCEPT the argument from illusion, or the supporting bit of argument that we have just considered, at face value and without reservations. The arguments he has expounded, he says, need to be 'evaluated', and the evaluation of them is what he next undertakes.[1] We must consider what he says.

Well, first we must regretfully note that Ayer swallows without hesitation a great deal in the argument that is highly objectionable; he accepts, in fact, all the really important blunders on which the argument rests. For example, he is not at all uneasy about the supposed dichotomy between 'sense-data' and 'material things'— he is inclined to argue about what *kind* of dichotomy this is, but that there *is* such a dichotomy he does not question; he does not jib at the unexplained introduction of these allegedly ubiquitous entities, 'perceptions', nor at the further dichotomy of these, with seeming neatness, into two groups, 'veridical' and 'delusive'; he accepts, further, without complaint the allegation that members of these two groups are not 'qualitatively distinguishable'. His position as to the merits of our ordinary, unamended, pre-philosophical manner of speaking is somewhat more

---

[1] Ayer, op. cit., pp. 11–19.

equivocal; on pp. 15–16 he seems to be saying that we really *are* involved in contradictions if certain 'assumptions' are made which certainly (to understate the case) we all do make, but on p. 31 he appears to retract this—there is, he there allows, no contradiction in our ordinary practice of taking some 'perceptions' to be 'veridical' and others not. But however this may be, he is at any rate ultimately persuaded that a 'technical terminology of some kind' is 'desirable'.

If, then, Ayer accepts so much of what the argument from illusion turns on, what exactly are the reservations that he wishes to make? Well, his main point—by now, no doubt, pretty well known—is that the issue raised is *not factual but linguistic*. He expresses, in fact, doubts as to whether the argument really works, even if it is taken to be concerned with a matter of fact; he doubts, at any rate, whether it could be taken as establishing that in fact we *always* perceive sense-data, since he is not clear (rightly enough) why 'perceptions of objects of different types' should *not* be 'qualitatively indistinguishable', or 'capable of being ranged in a continuous series'.[1] But further, he asks, 'Does the argument prove even that there are *any* cases of perception in which such a belief [*sc.* that the objects we directly perceive are material things] would be mistaken?'

It seems pretty odd, of course, to suggest that any argument is needed to prove this belief mistaken; for how in fact could anyone possibly suppose it to be true that

---

[1] I again omit the argument about 'causal dependence'.

what he perceives is *always* a 'material thing'? However, I think that this crack can be papered over. Ayer here, I think, has merely fallen into one of the traps which his own terminology sets for him, by taking it for granted that the *only alternative* to 'perceiving sense-data' is 'perceiving material things'; thus, in place of the absurdity of seeming to take seriously the idea that we *always* perceive material things, we can plausibly impute to him the more rational intention of raising the question whether we *ever* perceive sense-data. 'We never perceive sense-data' is not, as a matter of fact, equivalent to and interchangeable with 'We always perceive material things'; but Ayer pretty clearly *treats* these as interchangeable, and thus we can safely take it that the question he is now asking is: Does the argument from illusion really prove that, in any situations at all, we perceive sense-data?

His further argument on this point is not at all easy to follow, but it seems to go like this. (1) We have to admit— at least he appears to concede this—that sometimes we perceive 'sense-data which are not parts of any material things', if, but *only* if, we are prepared to allow that 'some perceptions are delusive'. (Of course all this won't really do, but we may let it pass for the moment.) But (2) do we *have* to allow that some perceptions are delusive? It is argued that we do, since otherwise 'we shall have to attribute to material things such mutually incompatible properties as being at the same time both green and yellow, or both elliptical and round'. But (3) such attributions, he says, yield contradictions only if 'certain assumptions' are made— for example that the 'real shape' of a penny remains the same when I change the point of view from which I look at it, that the temperature of water in a bowl is 'really the same' when I feel it first with a warm and then with a cold hand, or that an oasis 'does not really exist' at a certain place if no one except a crazed wanderer in the desert thinks that he sees one there. These 'assumptions', Ayer would presumably grant, look plausible enough; but why, he now says, shouldn't we just try denying them, all the same? Why shouldn't we say that material things are much spryer than we've been giving them credit for—constantly busy, from moment to moment, in changing their real shapes, colours, temperatures, sizes, and everything else? Why shouldn't we say, too, that they are much more numerous than is commonly thought—that, for instance, when I offer you (what we usually call) *a* cigarette, there are really *two* material things (two *cigarettes*?), one that I see and offer *and* one that you see and accept, if you do? 'I have no doubt', Ayer says, 'that by postulating a greater number of material things and regarding them as being more variable and evanescent than we normally do, it would be possible to deal with all the other cases in a similar way.'

Now Ayer seems to be right here—indeed, to be understating the case. If we allow ourselves this degree of *insouciant* latitude, surely we shall be able to deal—in *a way*, of course—with absolutely anything. But is there not something wrong with a solution on these lines? Well, I must here quote Ayer's own words: 'How then is one who holds this position to be refuted? The answer is that so long as we persist in regarding the issue as one concerning a matter of fact it is impossible for us to refute him. We cannot refute him, because, as far as the facts are concerned, there is really no dispute between us. . . . Where we say that the real shape of a coin is unchanging, he prefers to say that its shape is really undergoing some cyclical process of change. Where we say that two observers are seeing the same material thing, he prefers to say that they are seeing different things which have, however, some structural properties in common. . . . If there is here to be any question of truth or falsehood, there must be some disagreement about the nature of the empirical facts. And in this case no such disagreement exists.' Therefore, the question to which the argument from illusion purports to provide an answer is a purely *linguistic* question, not a question of fact: it has to do not with what is the case, but with how we are to talk. With this, Ayer concludes his 'evaluation' of the argument.

The main comment that I want to make on these pretty astonishing propositions concerns in particular the idea Ayer here seems to put forward, that the words 'real', 'really', 'real shape', 'real colour', &c., can perfectly well be used to mean *whatever you like*; and I shall also discuss what he says about what they do mean. But first I should like to point out the highly interesting fact that his way of 'proving' that the whole issue is purely verbal actually shows (what I am sure in any case is quite true) that he does not regard it as really verbal at all—his real view is that *in fact* we perceive only sense-data. This can quite easily be seen. One might at first sight be inclined to say that, if Ayer were right here, then absolutely every dispute would be purely verbal. For if, when one person says whatever it may be, another person may simply 'prefer to say' something else, they will *always* be arguing only about words, about what terminology is to be preferred. How could *anything* be a question of truth or falsehood, if anyone can always say whatever he likes? But here, of course, Ayer answers that, sometimes at least, there *is* real 'disagreement about the nature of the empirical facts'. But what kind of disagreement can this be? It is not, he says, (surprising as this may seem) a question of fact whether a penny, or any other 'material thing', does or does not constantly change its shape, its colour, its size, its location—here indeed we *can* say whatever we please. Where then are 'empirical facts' to be found? And Ayer's answer is quite clear—they are *facts about sense-data*, or as he also puts it, 'about the nature of the sensible appearances', 'the phenomena'; this is where we really encounter 'the empirical evidence'. There are in his view—his *real* view—no other 'empirical facts' at all. *The* hard fact is that there are sense-data; these entities really exist and are what they are; what other entities we may care to *speak as if* there were is a pure matter of verbal convenience, but 'the facts to which these expressions are intended to refer' will always be the same, facts about sense-data.

It thus becomes clear, not very surprisingly perhaps,

that the apparent sophistication of Ayer's 'linguistic' doctrine really rests squarely on the old Berkeleian, Kantian ontology of the 'sensible manifold'. He has all along, it seems, really been completely convinced by the very arguments that he purports to 'evaluate' with so much detachment. And there can be little doubt that this is owing in large measure to his wholesale acceptance of the traditional, time-hallowed, and disastrous manner of expounding them.[1]

It is a curious and in some ways rather melancholy fact that the relative positions of Price and Ayer at this point turn out to be exactly the same as the relative positions of Locke and Berkeley, or Hume and Kant. In Locke's view there are 'ideas' and also 'external objects', in Hume's 'impressions' and also 'external objects', in Price's view 'sense-data' and also 'physical occupants'; in Berkeley's doctrine there are *only* ideas, in Kant's only *Vorstellungen* (things-in-themselves being not strictly relevant here), in Ayer's doctrine there are *only* sense-data—but Berkeley, Kant, and Ayer all further agree that we can *speak as if* there were bodies, objects, material things. Certainly, Berkeley and Kant are not so liberal as Ayer—they don't suggest that, so long as we keep in step with the sensible manifold, we can talk exactly as we please; but on this issue, if I had to take sides, I think I should side with them.

[1] Or can there? One might also take the, in some ways, more charitable view that his off-hand treatment of the argument from illusion is due to his already being convinced *on other grounds* of what it purports to prove. I suspect there is a good deal in this, and we shall return to it later.

# VII

BUT NOW, PROVOKED LARGELY BY THE frequent and unexamined occurrences of 'real', 'really', 'real shape', &c., in the arguments we have just been considering, I want to take a closer look at this little word 'real'. I propose, if you like, to discuss the Nature of Reality—a genuinely important topic, though in general I don't much like making this claim.

There are two things, first of all, which it is immensely important to understand here.

1. 'Real' is an absolutely *normal* word, with nothing new-fangled or technical or highly specialized about it. It is, that is to say, already firmly established in, and very frequently used in, the ordinary language we all use every day. Thus *in this sense* it is a word which has a fixed meaning, and so can't, any more than can any other word which is firmly established, be fooled around with *ad lib*. Philosophers often seem to think that they can just 'assign' any meaning whatever to any word; and so no doubt, in an absolutely trivial sense, they can (like Humpty-Dumpty). There are some expressions, of course, 'material thing' for example, which only philosophers use, and in such cases they can, within reason, please themselves; but most words are *in fact* used in a

particular way already, and this fact can't be just disregarded. (For example, some meanings that have been assigned to 'know' and 'certain' have made it seem outrageous that we should use these terms as we actually do; but what this shows is that the meanings assigned by some philosophers are *wrong*.) Certainly, when we have discovered how a word is in fact used, that may not be the end of the matter; there is certainly no reason why, in general, things should be left exactly as we find them; we may wish to tidy the situation up a bit, revise the map here and there, draw the boundaries and distinctions rather differently. But still, it is advisable always to bear in mind (*a*) that the distinctions embodied in our vast and, for the most part, relatively ancient stock of ordinary words are neither few nor always very obvious, and almost never just arbitrary; (*b*) that in any case, before indulging in any tampering on our own account, we need to find out what it is that we have to deal with; and (*c*) that tampering with words in what we take to be one little corner of the field is always *liable* to have unforeseen repercussions in the adjoining territory. Tampering, in fact, is not so easy as is often supposed, is not justified or needed so often as is often supposed, and is often thought to be necessary just because what we've got already has been misrepresented. And we must always be particularly wary of the philosophical habit of dismissing some (if not all) the ordinary uses of a word as 'unimportant', a habit which makes distortion practically unavoidable. For instance, if we are going to talk about 'real', we must not dismiss as beneath contempt such humble but familiar expressions as 'not real cream'; this may save us from saying, for example, or seeming to say that what is not real cream must be a fleeting product of our cerebral processes.

2. The other immensely important point to grasp is that 'real' is *not* a normal word at all, but highly exceptional; exceptional in this respect that, unlike 'yellow' or 'horse' or 'walk', it does not have one single, specifiable, always-the-same *meaning*. (Even Aristotle saw through this idea.) *Nor* does it have a large number of different meanings—it is not *ambiguous*, even 'systematically'. Now words of this sort have been responsible for a great deal of perplexity. Consider the expressions 'cricket ball', 'cricket bat', 'cricket pavilion', 'cricket weather'. If someone did not know about cricket and were obsessed with the use of such 'normal' words as 'yellow', he might gaze at the ball, the bat, the building, the weather, trying to detect the 'common quality' which (he assumes) is attributed to these things by the prefix 'cricket'. But no such quality meets his eye; and so perhaps he concludes that 'cricket' must designate a *non-natural* quality, a quality to be detected not in any ordinary way but by *intuition*. If this story strikes you as too absurd, remember what philosophers have said about the word 'good'; and reflect that many philosophers, failing to detect any ordinary quality common to real ducks, real cream, and real progress, have decided that Reality must be an *a priori* concept apprehended by reason alone.

Let us begin, then, with a preliminary, no doubt rather haphazard, survey of some of the complexities in the use of 'real'. Consider, for instance, a case which at first sight one might think was pretty straightforward—the case of 'real colour'. What is meant by the 'real' colour of a thing? Well, one may say with some confidence, that's easy enough: the *real* colour of the thing is the colour that it looks to a normal observer in conditions of normal or standard illumination; and to find out what a thing's real colour is, we just need to be normal and to observe it in those conditions.

But suppose (*a*) that I remark to you of a third party, 'That isn't the real colour of her hair.' Do I mean by this that, if you were to observe her in conditions of standard illumination, you would find that her hair did not look that colour? Plainly not—the conditions of illumination may be standard already. I mean, of course, that her hair has been *dyed*, and normal illumination just doesn't come into it at all. Or suppose that you are looking at a ball of wool in a shop, and I say, 'That's not its real colour.' Here I *may* mean that it won't look that colour in ordinary daylight; but I *may* mean that wool isn't that colour before it's dyed. As so often, you can't tell what I mean just from the words that I use; it makes a difference, for instance, whether the thing under discussion is or is not of a type which is *customarily* dyed.

Suppose (*b*) that there is a species of fish which looks vividly multi-coloured, slightly glowing perhaps, at a depth of a thousand feet. I ask you what its real colour is.

So you catch a specimen and lay it out on deck, making sure the condition of the light is just about normal, and you find that it looks a muddy sort of greyish white. Well, is *that* its real colour? It's clear enough at any rate that we don't have to say so. In fact, is there any right answer in such a case?

Compare: 'What is the real taste of saccharine?' We dissolve a tablet in a cup of tea and we find that it makes the tea taste sweet; we then take a tablet neat, and we find that it tastes bitter. Is it *really* bitter, or *really* sweet?

(*c*) What is the real colour of the sky? Of the sun? Of the moon? Of a chameleon? We say that the sun in the evening sometimes looks red—well, what colour is it *really*? (What are the 'conditions of standard illumination' for the sun?)

(*d*) Consider a *pointilliste* painting of a meadow, say; if the general effect is of green, the painting may be composed of predominantly blue and yellow dots. What is the real colour of the painting?

(*e*) What is the real colour of an after-image? The trouble with this one is that we have no idea what an alternative to its 'real colour' might be. Its apparent colour, the colour that it looks, the colour that it appears to be?—but these phrases have no application here. (You might ask me, 'What colour is it really?' if you suspected that I had lied in telling you its colour. But 'What colour is it really?' is not quite the same as 'What is its real colour?')

Or consider 'real shape' for a moment. This notion cropped up, you may remember, seeming quite unproblematic, when we were considering the coin which was said to 'look elliptical' from some points of view; it had a real shape, we insisted, which remained unchanged. But coins in fact are rather special cases. For one thing their outlines are well defined and very highly stable, and for another they have a *known* and a *nameable* shape. But there are plenty of things of which this is not true. What is the real shape of a cloud? And if it be objected, as I dare say it could be, that a cloud is not a 'material thing' and so not the kind of thing which has to have a real shape, consider this case: what is the real shape of a cat? Does its real shape change whenever it moves? If not, in what posture *is* its real shape on display? Furthermore, is its real shape such as to be fairly smooth-outlined, or must it be finely enough serrated to take account of each hair? It is pretty obvious that there is *no* answer to these questions—no rules according to which, no procedure by which, answers are to be determined. Of course, there are plenty of shapes which the cat definitely is not—cylindrical, for instance. But only a desperate man would toy with the idea of ascertaining the cat's real shape 'by elimination'.

Contrast this with cases in which we *do* know how to proceed: 'Are those real diamonds?', 'Is that a real duck?' Items of jewellery that more or less closely resemble diamonds may not be real diamonds because they are paste or glass; that may not be a real duck because it is a decoy, or a toy duck, or a species of goose closely resembling a duck, or because I am having a hallucination. These are all of course quite different cases. And notice in particular (*a*) that, in most of them 'observation by a normal observer in standard conditions' is completely irrelevant; (*b*) that something which is not a real duck is not a *non-existent* duck, or indeed a non-existent anything; and (*c*) that something existent, e.g. a toy, may perfectly well not be real, e.g. not a real duck.[1]

Perhaps by now we have said enough to establish that there is more in the use of 'real' than meets the cursory eye; it has many and diverse uses in many diverse contexts. We must next, then, try to tidy things up a little; and I shall now mention under four headings what might be called the salient features of the use of 'real'—though not *all* these features are equally conspicuous in all its uses.

1. First, 'real' is a word that we may call *substantive-hungry*. Consider:

'These diamonds are real';
'These are real diamonds'.

This pair of sentences looks like, in an obvious grammatical respect, this other pair:

'These diamonds are pink';
'These are pink diamonds'.

---

[1] 'Exist', of course, is itself extremely tricky. The word is a verb, but it does not describe something that things do all the time, like breathing, only quieter—ticking over, as it were, in a metaphysical sort of way. It is only too easy to start wondering what, then, existing *is*. The Greeks were worse off than we are in this region of discourse—for our different expressions 'to be', 'to exist', and 'real' they made do with the single word εἶναι. We have not their excuse for getting confused on this admittedly confusing topic.

But whereas we can *just* say of something 'This is pink', we can't *just* say of something 'This is real'. And it is not very difficult to see why. We can perfectly well say of something that it is pink without knowing, without any reference to, what it *is*. But not so with 'real'. For one and the same object may be both a real *x* and not a real *y*; an object looking rather like a duck may be a real decoy duck (not just a toy) but not a real duck. When it isn't a real duck but a hallucination, it may still be a real hallucination—as opposed, for instance, to a passing quirk of a vivid imagination. That is, we must have an answer to the question 'A real *what*?', if the question 'Real or not?' is to have a definite sense, to get any foothold. And perhaps we should also mention here another point— that the question 'Real or not?' does not always come up, can't always be raised. We *do* raise this question only when, to speak rather roughly, suspicion assails us—in some way or other things may be not what they seem; and we *can* raise this question only if there *is* a way, or ways, in which things may be not what they seem. What alternative is there to being a 'real' after-image?

'Real' is not, of course, the only word we have that is substantive-hungry. Other examples, perhaps better known ones, are 'the same' and 'one'. The same *team* may not be the same *collection of players*; a body of troops may be one *company* and also three *platoons*. Then what about 'good'? We have here a variety of gaps crying out for substantives—'A good *what*?', 'Good *at* what?'—a good book, perhaps, but not a good novel; good at pruning roses, but not good at mending cars.[1]

2. Next, 'real' is what we may call a *trouser-word*. It is usually thought, and I dare say usually rightly thought, that what one might call the affirmative use of a term is basic—that, to understand '*x*', we need to know what it is to be *x*, or to be an *x*, and that knowing this apprises us of what it is *not* to be *x*, not to be an *x*. But with 'real' (as we briefly noted earlier) it is the *negative* use that wears the trousers. That is, a definite sense attaches to the assertion that something is real, a real such-and-such, only in the light of a specific way in which it might be, or might have been, *not* real. 'A real duck' differs from the simple 'a duck' only in that it is used to exclude various ways of being not a real duck—but a dummy, a toy, a picture, a decoy, &c.; and moreover I don't know *just* how to take the assertion that it's a real duck unless I know *just* what, on that particular occasion, the speaker has it in mind to exclude. This, of course, is why the attempt to find a characteristic common to all things that are or could be called 'real' is doomed to failure; the function of 'real' is not to contribute positively to the characterization of anything, but to exclude possible ways of being *not* real—and these ways are both numerous for particular kinds of things, and liable to be quite different for things of different kinds. It is this identity of

---

[1] In Greek the case of σοφός is of some importance; Aristotle seems to get into difficulties by trying to use σοφία 'absolutely', so to speak, without specification of the field in which σοφία is exercised and shown. Compare on δεινότης too.

general function combined with immense diversity in specific applications which gives to the word 'real' the, at first sight, baffling feature of having neither one single 'meaning', nor yet ambiguity, a number of different meanings.

3. Thirdly, 'real' is (like 'good') a *dimension-word*. I mean by this that it is the most general and comprehensive term in a whole group of terms of the same kind, terms that fulfil the same function. Other members of this group, on the affirmative side, are, for example, 'proper', 'genuine', 'live', 'true', 'authentic', 'natural'; and on the negative side, 'artificial', 'fake', 'false', 'bogus', 'makeshift', 'dummy', 'synthetic', 'toy'—and such nouns as 'dream', 'illusion', 'mirage', 'hallucination' belong here as well.[1] It is worth noticing here that, naturally enough, the *less* general terms on the affirmative side have the merit, in many cases, of suggesting more or less definitely what it is that is being excluded; they tend to pair off, that is, with particular terms on the negative side and thus, so to speak, to narrow the range of possibilities. If I say that I wish the university had a proper theatre, this suggests that it has at present a *makeshift* theatre; pictures are genuine as opposed to *fake*, silk is natural as opposed to *artificial*, ammunition is live as opposed to *dummy*, and so on. In practice, of course, we often get a clue to what it is that is in question from the substantive

[1] Of course, not all the uses of all these words are of the kind we are here considering—though it would be wise not to assume, either, that any of their uses are *completely* different, *completely* unconnected.

in the case, since we frequently have a well-founded antecedent idea in what respects the kind of thing mentioned could (and could not) be 'not real'. For instance, if you ask me 'Is this real silk?' I shall tend to supply 'as opposed to artificial', since I already know that silk is the kind of thing which can be very closely simulated by an artificial product. The notion of its being *toy* silk, for instance, will not occur to me.[1]

A large number of questions arises here—which I shall not go into—concerning both the composition of these families of 'reality'-words and 'unreality'-words, and also the distinctions to be drawn between their individual members. Why, for instance, is being a *proper* carving-knife one way of being a real carving-knife, whereas being *pure* cream seems not to be one way of being *real* cream? Or to put it differently: how does the distinction between real cream and synthetic cream differ from the distinction between pure cream and adulterated cream? Is it just that adulterated cream still is, after all, *cream*? And why are false teeth called 'false' rather than, say, 'artificial'? Why are artificial limbs so-called, in *preference* to 'false'? Is it that false teeth, besides doing much the same job as real teeth, look, and are meant to look, *deceptively* like real teeth? Whereas an artificial limb, perhaps, is meant to do

---

[1] Why not? Because silk can't be 'toy'. Yes, but why not? Is it that a toy is, strictly speaking, something quite small, and specially made or designed to be manipulated in play? The water in toy beer-bottles is not toy beer, but *pretend* beer. Could a toy watch actually have clockwork inside and show the time correctly? Or would that be just a *miniature* watch?

the same job, but is neither intended, nor likely, to be *passed off* as a real limb.

Another philosophically notorious dimension-word, which has already been mentioned in another connexion as closely comparable with 'real', is 'good'. 'Good' is the most general of a very large and diverse list of more specific words, which share with it the general function of expressing commendation, but differ among themselves in their aptness to, and implications in, particular contexts. It is a curious point, of which Idealist philosophers used to make much at one time, that 'real' itself, in certain uses, may belong to this family. 'Now this is a *real* carving-knife!' may be one way of saying that this is a good carving-knife.[1] And it is sometimes said of a bad poem, for instance, that it isn't really a poem at all; a certain standard must be reached, as it were, even to *qualify*.

4. Lastly, 'real' also belongs to a large and important family of words that we may call *adjuster-words*—words, that is, by the use of which other words are adjusted to meet the innumerable and unforeseeable demands of the world upon language. The position, considerably over-simplified no doubt, is that at a given time our language contains words that enable us (more or less) to say what we want to say in most situations that (we think) are liable to turn up. But vocabularies are finite; and the variety of possible situations that may confront us is

---

[1] Colloquially at least, the converse is also found: 'I gave him a good hiding'—'a real hiding'—'a proper hiding'.

neither finite nor precisely foreseeable. So situations are practically bound to crop up sometimes with which our vocabulary is not already fitted to cope in any tidy, straightforward style. We have the word 'pig', for instance, and a pretty clear idea which animals, among those that we fairly commonly encounter, are and are not to be so called. But one day we come across a new kind of animal, which looks and behaves very much as pigs do, but not *quite* as pigs do; it is somehow different. Well, we might just keep silent, not knowing what to say; we don't want to say positively that it *is* a pig, or that it is *not*. Or we might, if for instance we expected to want to refer to these new creatures pretty often, invent a quite new word for them. But what we could do, and probably would do first of all, is to say, 'It's *like* a pig.' ('Like' is *the* great adjuster-word, or, alternatively put, the main flexibility-device by whose aid, in spite of the limited scope of our vocabulary, we can always avoid being left completely speechless.) And then, having said of this animal that it's *like* a pig, we may proceed with the remark, 'But it isn't a *real* pig'—or more specifically, and using a term that naturalists favour, 'not a *true* pig'. If we think of words as being shot like arrows at the world, the function of these adjuster-words is to free us from the disability of being able to shoot only straight ahead; by their use on occasion, such words as 'pig' can be, so to speak, brought into connexion with targets lying slightly off the simple, straightforward line on which they are ordinarily aimed. And in this way we gain, besides flexibility, precision; for if I can say, 'Not a real pig, but like a pig', I don't have to tamper with the meaning of 'pig' itself.

But, one might ask, do we *have* to have 'like' to serve this purpose? We have, after all, other flexibility-devices. For instance, I might say that animals of this new species are 'piggish'; I might perhaps call them 'quasi-pigs', or describe them ( in the style of vendors of peculiar wines) as 'pig-type' creatures. But these devices, excellent no doubt in their way, can't be regarded as substitutes for 'like', for this reason: they equip us simply with new expressions on the same level as, functioning in the same way as, the word 'pig' itself; and thus, though they may perhaps help us out of our immediate difficulty, they themselves may land us in exactly the same *kind* of difficulty at any time. We have this kind of wine, not real port, but a tolerably close approximation to port, and we call it 'port type'. But then someone produces a new kind of wine, not port exactly, but also not quite the same as what we now call 'port type'. So what are we to say? Is it port-type type? It would be tedious to have to say so, and besides there would clearly be no future in it. But as it is we can say that it is *like* port-type wine (and for that matter rather like port, too); and in saying this we don't saddle ourselves with a *new word*, whose application may itself prove problematic if the vintners spring yet another surprise on us. The word 'like' equips us *generally* to handle the unforeseen, in a way in which new words invented *ad hoc* don't, and can't.

(Why then do we need 'real' as an adjuster-word as well as 'like'? Why exactly do we want to say, sometimes 'It is like a pig', sometimes 'It is not a real pig'? To answer these questions properly would be to go a long way towards making really clear the use, the 'meaning', of 'real'.)[1]

It should be quite clear, then, that there are no criteria to be laid down *in general* for distinguishing the real from the not real. How this is to be done must depend on *what* it is with respect to which the problem arises in particular cases. Furthermore, even for particular kinds of things, there may be many different ways in which the distinction may be made (there is not just *one* way of being 'not a real pig')—this depends on the number and variety of the surprises and dilemmas nature and our fellow men may spring on us, and on the surprises and dilemmas we have been faced with hitherto. And of course, if there is *never* any dilemma or surprise, the question simply doesn't come up; if we had simply never had occasion to distinguish anything as being in any way like a pig but not a *real* pig, then the words 'real pig' themselves would have no application—as perhaps the words 'real after-image' have no application.

Again, the criteria we employ at a given time can't be taken as *final*, not liable to change. Suppose that one day a creature of the kind we now call a cat takes to talking.

---

[1] Incidentally, nothing is gained at all by saying that 'real' is a *normative* word and leaving it at that, for 'normative' itself is much too general and vague. Just how, in what way, is 'real' normative? Not, presumably, in just the same way as 'good' is. And it's the differences that matter.

Well, we say to begin with, I suppose, 'This cat can talk.' But then other cats, not all, take to talking as well; we now have to say that some cats talk, we distinguish between talking and non-talking cats. But again we may, if talking becomes prevalent and the distinction between talking and not talking seems to us to be really important, come to insist that a *real* cat be a creature that can talk. And this will give us a new case of being 'not a real cat', i.e. being a creature just like a cat except for not talking.

Of course—this may seem perhaps hardly worth saying, but in philosophy it seems it does need to be said—we make a distinction between 'a real $x$' and 'not a real $x$' only if there is a way of telling the difference between what is a real $x$ and what is not. A distinction which we are not in fact able to draw is—to put it politely—not worth making.

# VIII

TO RETURN NOW TO AYER. WE HAVE ALready entered a protest against his apparent belief that 'real' is a word that can be used in any way one likes—that though some say, for instance, the real shape of a building remains the same as one views it from different standpoints, one may quite well 'prefer to say' that its real shape constantly changes. But now I want to consider the last section of his book, which is called 'Appearance and Reality',[1] and in which he undertakes to give an account of the distinction as we ordinarily make it. He regards this, I suppose, as a description of our 'preferences'.

Ayer begins by making a distinction between 'perceptions' which are 'qualitatively delusive' and 'existentially delusive'. In the first case we are said to find that 'the sense-data endow material things with qualities that they do not really possess', in the second that 'the material things that they seem to present do not exist at all'. However, this distinction is, to say the least, unclear. The expression 'existentially delusive' puts one in mind, naturally enough, of cases in which one is actually *deluded*—in which, for instance, one thinks one sees an oasis but an oasis 'does not exist at all'; and it is this sort

[1] Ayer, op. cit., pp. 263-74.

of case that Ayer evidently has in mind. The phrase 'qualitatively delusive', on the other hand, is evidently meant to apply in cases where some object is certainly before us, no doubt about that, but one of its 'qualities' is under suspicion—it looks blue for instance, but is it *really* blue? Now it seems to be implied that these two types of cases exhaust the field. But do they? Suppose that I see a decoy duck and take it for a real duck; in which of Ayer's ways is my 'perception' to be said to be 'delusive'? Well, it just isn't clear. It might be held to be 'qualitatively' delusive, as endowing the material thing with 'qualities that it does not really possess'; for example, I mistakenly suppose that the object I see could quack. But then again it might be said to be 'existentially' delusive, since the material thing it seems to present does not exist; I think there is a real duck before me but in fact there isn't. So Ayer's initial distinction presents us with false alternatives; it suggests that we have just two cases to consider, in one of which the only question is whether the thing we perceive really has the 'quality' it seems to have, and in the other of which the only question is whether the thing which we seem to perceive does really exist. But in the case of the decoy duck this breaks down at once; and there are plenty of other such cases. It looks as though, in trying to make this initial distinction, Ayer has frozen on to the truly 'delusive' sort of case, in which I think I see something where *nothing* really is, and has simply overlooked the much more common case in which I think I see something where something *else* really is.

As a result a large part, and probably the largest part, of the territory within which we draw distinctions between 'appearance and reality' is completely omitted from his discussion. He discusses (very briefly indeed) the case in which something is or might be taken to exist when it does not really exist at all; he discusses at rather greater length the case in which something is or might be supposed to have a characteristic which it does not really have; but he simply doesn't mention the very numerous and very various cases in which something is or might be taken *to be* what it isn't really—as paste diamonds, for instance, may be taken to be real diamonds. The distinction between 'qualitative' and 'existential' delusion doesn't properly apply to these cases, but then that is *just* what is wrong with the distinction. It divides up the topic in a way that leaves a lot of it out.[1]

However, Ayer undertakes as his major enterprise to 'furnish an explanation of the use of the word "real" as it is applied to the characteristics of material things'. The distinction here between being 'delusive' and being 'veridical', he says, 'does not depend upon a difference in the intrinsic qualities of sense-data', since an elliptical sense-datum could, after all, just as well 'present' something really elliptical as something really round; so the distinction 'must depend upon a difference in their relations', namely their relations to other sense-data.

---

[1] One might add that a good deal is arbitrarily excluded by Ayer's restriction of his discussion to questions about 'material things'—unless, which I doubt, he could classify as material *things* such *stuffs* as silk, glass, gold, cream, &c. And couldn't I raise the question 'Is that a real rainbow?'

One might try, Ayer says, to identify a sense-datum as 'a bearer of the real character of the relevant material thing' by saying that such a sense-datum is what occurs 'in what are conventionally taken to be preferential conditions'. However, he objects to this on two grounds; first, 'that these preferential conditions are not the same for every kind of material thing',[1] and second, that it is surely necessary to explain *why* certain conditions should be selected as 'preferential'. This explanation Ayer now gives and elaborates. 'The privileged sense-data', he says, i.e. those which present the 'real qualities' of material things, 'are found to be the most reliable members of the groups to which they belong, in the sense that they have the greatest value as sources of prediction.' He later adds as meritorious features what he calls 'sensible constancy', and measurability; but here too it is really, he thinks, *predictive value* which determines the ascription of reality. For example; if I am *very* close to an object, or *very* far away from it, I am pretty badly placed for predicting 'how it will look' from other points of view, whereas, if I view it from a more moderate distance, I may be able to tell quite well 'how it will look' from closer to, or further away. (It is not quite clear what characteristic of the object is in question here, but it seems to be shape that is meant.) So, the argument goes, we say that the 'real shape' is the shape the thing looks at the more moderate range. Again, if I look at an object through dark glasses, it may be hard to tell what colour

[1] It's interesting that Ayer should feel this to be an *objection*.

it will look when I take them off; hence, through dark glasses, we say, it doesn't look its 'real colour'.

However, this will not do as a *general* account even of the very restricted bit of the use of 'real' which Ayer chooses to discuss. (The important point is, in fact, just that there *is* no general account, and Ayer is chasing a will-o'-the-wisp in trying to find one.) For consider some questions about 'real' colour. Here there are *many* cases of a kind which Ayer, generalizing on the basis of one example, takes no account of. Some we have already mentioned. For instance, 'That's not the real colour of her hair.' Why not? Because the colour her hair now looks is an unreliable basis for prediction? Because the colour her hair now looks is not 'most conspicuously differentiated' from the other constituents of my sense-field? No. That's not the real colour of her hair because she's *dyed* it. Or suppose that I have grown a specimen of what is normally a white flower in an appropriately constituted green fluid, so that its petals are now a pale shade of green: I say, 'Of course, that's not its real colour.' Why do I say this? I can, after all, make all the standard predictions about how my specimen will look in various conditions. But my reason for saying that pale green is not its real colour has nothing at all to do with that; it is simply that the flower's *natural* colour is white. And there are some cases, involving no artificial interference with things, which run directly counter to Ayer's doctrine. If I look very closely indeed at a piece of cloth I may see it as a criss-cross pattern of black and white, and be able to predict that from other points of view it will look grey; if I look at it from a range of several yards, it may look grey, and I may *not* be able to predict that, close to, it will look black and white; but we say, all the same, that its colour is grey. Then what about *taste*? If someone who isn't in the habit of drinking wine says of the glass I give him that it's sour, I might protest, 'It isn't really sour'—meaning thereby, not that the notion that it's sour will provide a poor basis for prediction, but that, if he savours it a bit more sympathetically, he'll realize that it just isn't *like* things that are sour, that his first reaction, though understandable perhaps, was inappropriate.

However, as I said, what is wrong in principle with Ayer's account of the use of 'real' is just that he is attempting to give *one* account—or two, if we include his perfunctory remarks on the 'existentially' delusive. In fact what he says is not generally true even of 'real colour'; and certainly it does not help us at all with real pearls, real ducks, real cream, real watches, real novels, and the rest—all those uses of 'real' which Ayer overlooks entirely. Just why it is a mistake to look for any single, quite general account of the use of the word 'real' has, I hope, been made clear enough already, and I shall not repeat it now. I should like to emphasize, however, how fatal it always is to embark on explaining the use of a word without seriously considering more than a tiny fraction of the contexts in which it is actually used. In this case, as in others, Ayer seems to be encouraged in the fatal enterprise by an initial propensity to believe that the terrain can be neatly and exhaustively divided in two.

# IX

ALL THIS LENGTHY DISCUSSION OF THE Nature of Reality arose, you may remember, out of the passage in which Ayer 'evaluates' the argument from illusion, arriving at the conclusion that the issue it raises is really not factual but linguistic. I argued earlier that his way of arriving at this conclusion actually shows that he does not believe it; for it relies on the doctrine that real 'empirical facts' are *in fact* always about 'sensible appearances', and that remarks ostensibly about 'material things' are to be *contrasted* as just a way of speaking—'the facts to which these expressions are intended to refer' are facts about 'phenomena', the only real facts there are. But however that may be, the official state of play at this point is that we are confronted with a linguistic question: are we *to say* that the objects we directly perceive are sense-data?—and that the argument from illusion has given us no compelling reason for choosing to say this. So Ayer next goes on himself to give the reasons why we should say this; and this section,[1] which is called 'The Introduction of Sense-data', must now be considered.

It is indeed true, Ayer says, that 'if we restrict ourselves to using words in such a way that to say of an

[1] Ayer, op. cit., pp. 19–28.

object that it is seen or touched or otherwise perceived entails saying that it really exists and that something really has the character that the object appears to have, we shall be obliged either to deny that any perceptions are delusive or else to admit that it is a mistake to speak as if the objects that we perceived were always material things'. But in fact we do not have to use words in this way. 'If I say that I am seeing a stick which looks crooked, I do not imply that anything really is crooked . . . or if, being subject to an illusion of double vision, I say that I am perceiving two pieces of paper, I need not be implying that there really are two pieces of paper there. But surely, it may be said, if the two pieces of paper really are perceived they must both exist in some sense, even if not as material things. The answer to this objection is that it is based on a misunderstanding of the way in which I am using the word "perceive". I am using it here in such a way that to say of an object that it is perceived does not entail saying that it exists in any sense at all. And this is a perfectly correct and familiar usage of the word.'

But, Ayer continues, 'there is also a correct and familiar usage of the word "perceive", in which to say of an object that it is perceived does carry the implication that it exists'. And if I use the word 'in this sense' in my case of double vision, I must say, 'I thought I perceived two pieces of paper but I was really perceiving only one.' 'If the word is used in one familiar sense, it can be said that I really did perceive two pieces of paper. If it is used in another sense, which is also sanctioned by convention,

*Sense and Sensibilia*

then it must be said that I perceived only one.' 'There is no problem so long as one keeps the two usages distinct.'[1]

Similarly, a man may say 'that he sees a distant star which has an extension greater than that of the earth'; he may also say that he is 'actually seeing ... a silvery speck no bigger than a sixpence'. And these remarks, Ayer says, are not inconsistent. For in *one sense* of 'see', 'it is necessary that what is seen should really exist, but not necessary that it should have the qualities that it appears to have'—in *this* sense the man sees an enormous star; but in *another sense*, 'it is not possible that anything should seem to have qualities that it does not really have, but also not necessary that what is seen should really exist'—in *this* sense the man 'can say truly that what he sees is no bigger than a sixpence'.

But what about sense-data? They are now brought in, in the following way. Some philosophers may decide, Ayer says, *both* 'to apply the word "see" or any other words that designate modes of perception to delusive as well as veridical experiences', and *also* (rather misguidedly, one might think) to use these words 'in such a way that what is seen or otherwise sensibly experienced must really exist and must really have the properties that it appears to have'. But then, naturally enough, they find that they can't say that 'what is experienced' is always a

[1] Price also thinks that 'perceive' is *ambiguous*, that it has *two senses*. Cp. *Perception*, p. 23. 'It is possible to perceive what does not exist. ... But in another sense of 'perceive', and one that comes closer to ordinary speech, it is not possible to perceive what does not exist.'

material thing; for in 'delusive' situations, either the thing doesn't 'really exist' or doesn't 'really have the properties that it appears to have'. And then, it seems— instead of having second thoughts about their use of 'see'—they decide to say that 'what is experienced' in 'delusive' situations is a *sense-datum*. Next, they find it 'convenient', Ayer says, 'to extend this usage to all cases', on the old, familiar ground that 'delusive and veridical perceptions' don't differ in 'quality'. This, Ayer says, 'can reasonably be accepted as a rule of language. And thus one arrives at the conclusion that in all cases of perception the objects of which one is directly aware are sense-data and not material things.' This procedure, Ayer says, does not embody 'any factual discovery'; it amounts to the recommendation of 'a new verbal usage'. And he for his part is disposed to adopt this recommendation; 'it does not in itself add to our knowledge of empirical facts, or even make it possible for us to express anything that we could not have expressed without it. At the best it enables us only to refer to familiar facts *in a clearer and more convenient way*.' My italics.

Now an important, or at any rate prominent, part of the argumentation which leads to this conclusion is the allegation that there are *different senses*, all (or is it only *some*?) 'correct and familiar', of 'perceive' and other verbs designating modes of perception.[1] Just what this

---

[1] Justice, I think, demands that I should reiterate here that a lot of water has flowed under the bridges since Ayer wrote his book. Doctrines

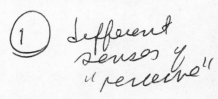

allegation has to do with the argument we shall have to consider in due course; but first, I want to look into the grounds on which it is made, and to ask whether it is well founded.

Let us look, then, at the examples in which these different senses are supposed to be exhibited. First, the familiar old case of the stick in water. Ayer says: 'If I say that I am seeing a stick which looks crooked, I do not imply that anything really is crooked.' Now this is quite true; but what does it show? It is evidently *meant* to show that there is *a sense* of 'see' in which to say that something is seen does not entail saying 'that it exists and that something really has the character that the object appears to have'. But the example surely does not show this at all. All that it *shows* is that the complete utterance 'I see a stick which looks crooked' does not entail that anything really is crooked. That this is so *in virtue of the sense in which 'see' is here used* is an additional step, for which no justification is given. And in fact, when one comes to think of it, this step is not only undefended, but pretty certainly wrong. For if one *had* to pick on some *part* of the utterance as that in virtue of which it doesn't entail that anything really is crooked, surely the phrase 'which looks crooked' would be the likeliest candidate. For whatever views we may or may not have about senses of 'see', we all know that what looks crooked may not really *be* crooked.

about supposed different senses of verbs of perception had been widely current in the decade or two before he was writing, and it is not very surprising that he should have taken them on as part of the stock-in-trade. No doubt he would not take exactly the same line today.

The second example is ineffective, off-target, in a rather similar way. Ayer says: 'If I say that someone is feeling pressure on his leg, I do not necessarily exclude the possibility that his leg has been amputated.' But again, why explain this by invoking *a sense* of 'feel'? Why not say instead, for instance, that the expression 'pressure on his leg' can sometimes be used to specify what someone feels, even if his leg has actually been amputated? It seems to me very doubtful whether we should say that there is exemplified here a special *sense* even of the words 'pressure on his leg'; but at any rate the case for saying this would be just as good as for saying we have here a special sense of 'feel'—in fact a good deal better.

The third example, of double vision, is less easily dealt with. Here Ayer says: 'If I say that I am perceiving two pieces of paper, I need not be implying that there really are two pieces of paper there.' Now this, I think, is true only with some qualification. It is, I suppose, true that, if I know that I am suffering from double vision, I may say 'I am perceiving two pieces of paper' and, in saying this, *not mean* that there really are two pieces of paper there; but for all that, I think, my utterance does imply that there are, in the sense that anyone not apprised of the special circumstances of the case would naturally and properly, in view of my utterance, suppose that I thought there were two pieces of paper. However, we may agree that in saying 'I am perceiving two pieces of paper', I may not *mean*—since I may know it to be untrue—that there really are two pieces of paper before me. So far, so good.

But in the next sentence Ayer changes the form of words; 'if two pieces of paper *really are perceived*', he says, it need not be true that there are two pieces of paper. And this is surely just wrong. In fact, that 'two pieces of paper *really are perceived*' is just what we should *not* say in a case of double vision—just for the reason that there must *be* two, if two 'really are perceived'.

But, it may be said, have we not conceded enough to justify the main point that Ayer is making here? For whatever the case may be with 'really are perceived', we have agreed that I may properly say, 'I am perceiving two pieces of paper', in the full knowledge that there are not really two pieces before me. And since it is undeniable that these words may *also* be so used as to imply that there really *are* two pieces of paper, do we not have to agree that there are two different senses of 'perceive'?

Well, no, we don't. The linguistic facts here adduced are not enough to prove anything like so much as this. For one thing, if there really were two *senses* of 'perceive', one would naturally expect that 'perceive' might occur in either of these senses in any of its constructions. But in fact, even if 'I perceive two pieces' needn't mean that there *are* two pieces, it seems that 'Two pieces really are perceived' is *not* compatible with there being really only one. So it looks as though it might be better to say that the implications of 'perceive' may differ in different *constructions* than just that there are two *senses* of 'perceive'. But more important than this is the fact that double vision is a quite *exceptional* case, so that we may have to stretch our ordinary usage to accommodate it. Since, in this exceptional situation, though there is only one piece of paper I seem to see two, I may want to say, 'I am perceiving two pieces of paper' *faute de mieux*, knowing quite well that the situation isn't really that in which these words are perfectly appropriate. But the fact that an exceptional situation may thus induce me to use words primarily appropriate for a different, normal situation is nothing like enough to establish that there are, in general, two different, normal ('correct and familiar') *senses* of the words I use, or of any one of them. To produce a rather baffling abnormality like double vision could establish only, at most, that ordinary usage sometimes has to be stretched to accommodate exceptional situations. It is not, as Ayer says, that 'there is no problem so long as one keeps the two usages distinct'; there is no reason to say that there *are* two usages; there is 'no problem' so long as one is aware of the *special circumstances*.

I might say, while visiting the zoo, 'That is a lion', pointing to one of the animals. I might also say, pointing to a photograph in my album, 'That is a lion.' Does this show that the word 'lion' has *two senses*—one meaning an animal, the other a picture of an animal? Plainly not. In order (in this case) to cut down verbiage, I may use in one situation words primarily appropriate to the other; and no problem arises provided the circumstances are known.

As a matter of fact, in the case of double vision, it is not true that my only resource is to stretch in the way envisaged the ordinary use of 'I am perceiving two pieces of paper.' Certainly I *might* do this; but in fact there is a special idiom, which Ayer might usefully have mentioned, for use in this special case—'I see the piece of paper double.' I might also say that I 'see it as two'.

Now let us consider the case of the man who sees a star, a case of which Ayer's account is particularly puzzling. The man is supposed, you remember, to say two things: (*a*) 'I see a distant star which has an extension greater than that of the earth'; and (*b*)—on being asked to describe what it is that he is actually seeing—'I see a silvery speck no bigger than a sixpence.' Ayer's first observation is that 'one is tempted to conclude that one at least of these assertions is false'. But *is* one? Why should one be? One might of course feel this temptation if one were in a state of extreme astronomical ignorance—if, that is, one thought that those silvery specks in the sky couldn't really be stars larger than the earth, or if, conversely, one thought that something larger than the earth, even though distant, couldn't really be seen as a silvery speck. But most of us know that stars are very, very big, and that they are a very, very long way away; we know what they *look* like to the naked and earthbound eye, and we know a bit at any rate about what they *are* like. Thus, I can't see any reason at all why we should be tempted to think that 'seeing an enormous star' is incompatible with 'seeing a silvery speck'. Wouldn't we be quite prepared to say, and quite correct in saying, that the silvery speck *is* a star?

Perhaps, though, this is not very important, since,

although Ayer surprisingly thinks we should feel this temptation, he also thinks that we ought to resist it; the man's two statements, he agrees, aren't really incompatible. And he goes on to explain this by saying 'that the word "see", like the word "perceive", is commonly used in a variety of senses'. There is one 'sense' in which it is true that the man sees a star, and another 'sense' in which it is true that he sees a silvery speck. Well, what are these senses?

'In one sense', Ayer says, 'the sense in which the man can say truly that he sees the star, it is necessary that what is seen should really exist, but not necessary that it should have the qualities that it appears to have.' This is probably all right, though in the context a bit obscure. We may accept that 'it is necessary that what is seen should really exist'; the difficulty with the other condition—'not necessary that it should have the qualities that it appears to have'—is that it is not made clear what, in the example, 'the qualities that it appears to have' are supposed to be. The general trend of the discussion suggests that *size* is meant. But if so there is the difficulty that the question 'What size does it appear *to be*?', asked of a star, is a question to which no sensible man would attempt to give an answer. He might indeed say that it 'looks tiny'; but it would be absurd to take this as meaning that it looks as if it *is* tiny, that it appears to *be* tiny. In the case of an object so immensely distant as a star, there is really no such thing as 'the size that it appears to be' when one looks at it, since there is no question of making that sort of estimate of its size. One couldn't sensibly say 'To judge from appearances, it's $\left\{\begin{array}{c}\text{smaller}\\\text{bigger}\end{array}\right\}$ than the earth', because appearances in fact provide no basis whatever even for so rough a judgement as this. However, we can perhaps patch things up by changing the example. Stars notoriously twinkle; and one could, I think, reasonably say in virtue of this that they *appear* to be intermittently, irregularly, or discontinuously luminous. Thus, if we take it that stars are not really discontinuously luminous, and we are prepared to say that we see stars, it can be concluded that we evidently do not require that what is seen should have 'the qualities that it appears to have'.

So now let us turn to Ayer's other 'sense'. 'In another sense', he says, 'which is that in which the man can truly say that what he sees is no bigger than a sixpence, it is not possible that anything should seem to have qualities that it does not really have, but also not necessary that what is seen should really exist.' Now perhaps this *would* be 'another sense' of 'see', if there were any such sense; but in fact there is *no* such 'sense' as this. If a man says 'I see a silvery speck', *of course* he 'implies' that the speck exists, that there is a speck; and if there is *no* speck in the region of the night sky at which he is looking, if that part of the sky is perfectly blank, then of course he does *not* see a silvery speck there. It is no use his saying, 'Well, that region of the sky may be perfectly blank, but it is still true that I see a silvery speck; for I am using "see" in such a sense that what is seen need not exist.' It might be thought, perhaps, that I am being unfair here; in saying that the speck the man sees need not 'really exist', it might be said, Ayer can't mean that there may be simply no speck to be seen—he just means that it needn't 'really exist' as the occupant of a definite region of physical space, as the star does. But no—Ayer certainly *does* mean just what I have taken him to mean; for you may remember that he said earlier, as explicitly as could be, that there is a 'correct and familiar' usage of 'perceive' which is such that 'to say of an object that it is perceived does not entail saying that it exists *in any sense at all*'. On this there is no possible comment except that there *isn't*.[1]

The other feature of this alleged sense of 'see' is hardly less peculiar. It is suggested that, in the 'sense' of 'see' in which the man sees a silvery speck, it is 'not possible that anything should seem to have qualities that it does not really have'. Here again it is not perfectly clear what qualities are meant; but it looks as if Ayer has in mind the 'quality' of *being no bigger than a sixpence*. But surely there is something rather absurd about this. Remember that we are talking here about the *speck*, not the star. And can the question whether the speck really *is* no bigger than a sixpence, or whether perhaps it just *seems* to be no

---

[1] What about seeing ghosts? Well, if I say that cousin Josephine once saw a ghost, even if I go on to say I don't 'believe in' ghosts, whatever that means, I can't say that ghosts don't exist *in any sense at all*. For there was, in *some* sense, this ghost that Josephine saw. If I do want to insist that ghosts don't exist *in any sense at all*, I can't afford to admit that people ever see them—I shall have to say that they think they do, that they seem to see them, or what not.

bigger than a sixpence, be seriously raised? What difference could there be between the supposed alternatives? To say 'It's no bigger than a sixpence' is itself nothing more, after all, than a rough-and-ready way of saying how it looks. But then, if we think instead of something that might *seriously* be taken to be a 'quality' of the speck—for instance, the quality of being pinkish in colour—we get the conclusion, once again, that there is no such sense of 'see' as Ayer is saying there is. For of course, when someone sees a speck in the night sky, it might, through some abnormality in the state of his eyes for instance, look greyish to him though it's really pinkish. The only way in which one can make it appear that something seen can't seem to have a quality that it really has not *is* to pick on something like 'being no bigger than a sixpence'—but in that case the impossibility is due, *not* to the 'sense' in which 'see' is being used, but to the absurdity of treating 'being no bigger than a sixpence' as if (in this context) it were a *quality* with respect to which it could make any sense at all to *distinguish* between really having it and only seeming to. The fact is that, just as there is *no* sense of 'see' which is such that what is seen need 'not exist in any sense at all', there is *no* sense of 'see', neither the same sense nor any other,[1] in which it is impossible that what is seen 'should

---

[1] It is in fact very hard to understand how Ayer could ever have thought he was characterizing a *single* sense of 'see' by this conjunction of conditions. For how could one possibly say, in the same breath, 'It must really have the qualities it seems to have', and 'It may not exist'? *What* must have the qualities it seems to have?

seem to have qualities that it does not really have'. I am not denying, of course, that we could arbitrarily invent such uses of 'see', though I don't know why we should want to; but it must be remembered that Ayer is purporting here to describe 'senses' of 'see' which are already 'correct', and even 'familiar'.

We have now come to the end of the examples which Ayer produces; and it appears that none of them gives any support to the idea that there are different 'senses' of 'perceive', 'see', and the rest. One of the examples— the one about double vision—does suggest, what in any case is only to be expected, that in exceptional situations ordinary forms of words may be used without being *meant* in quite the ordinary way; our saying of the D.T.'s sufferer that he 'sees pink rats' is a further instance of this, since we don't mean here (as would be meant in a normal situation) that there are real, live pink rats which he sees; but such stretchings of ordinary words in exceptional situations certainly do not constitute special *senses*, still less 'correct and familiar' senses, of the words in question. And the other examples either fail to be relevant to the question about different senses of these words, or, as in the star case as described by Ayer, bring in alleged 'senses' which quite certainly don't exist.

What has gone wrong, then? I think that part of what has gone wrong is this: observing, perfectly correctly, that the question 'What does X perceive?' can be given —normally at least—many different answers, and that these different answers may all be correct and therefore compatible, Ayer has jumped to the conclusion that 'perceive' must have different 'senses'—for if not, how could *different* answers to the question all be *correct*? But the proper explanation of the linguistic facts is not this at all; it is simply that what we 'perceive' can be described, identified, classified, characterized, named in many different ways. If I am asked 'What did you kick?', I might answer 'I kicked a piece of painted wood', or I might say 'I kicked Jones's front door'; both of these answers might well be correct; but should we say for that reason that 'kick' is used in them in different senses? Obviously not. What I kicked—in just one 'sense', the ordinary one—could be described as a piece of painted wood, *or* identified as Jones's front door; the piece of wood in question *was* Jones's front door. Similarly, I may say 'I see a silvery speck' or 'I see a huge star'; what I see— in the single, ordinary 'sense' this word has—can be described as a silvery speck, or identified as a very large star; for the speck in question *is* a very large star.[1]

Suppose you ask me 'What did you see this morning?'. I might answer, 'I saw a man shaved in Oxford.' Or again I might say, no less correctly and referring to the same occasion, 'I saw a man born in Jerusalem.' Does it follow that I must be using 'see' in different senses? Of course not. The plain fact is that two things are true of the man that I saw—(*a*) that he was being shaved in Oxford, and

---

[1] It doesn't follow, of course, that we could properly say, 'That very large star is a speck.' I might say, 'That white dot on the horizon is my house', but this would not license the conclusion that I live in a white dot.

(*b*) that he had been born some years earlier in Jerusalem. And certainly I can allude to either of these facts about him in saying—in *no* way ambiguously—that I saw him. Or if there *is* ambiguity here, it is not the word 'saw' that is ambiguous.

Suppose that I look through a telescope and you ask me, 'What do you see?'. I may answer (1) 'A bright speck'; (2) 'A star'; (3) 'Sirius'; (4) 'The image in the fourteenth mirror of the telescope.' All these answers may be perfectly correct. Have we then different senses of 'see'? *Four* different senses? Of course not. The image in the fourteenth mirror of the telescope *is* a bright speck, this bright speck *is* a star, and the star *is* Sirius; I can say, quite correctly and with no ambiguity whatever, that I see any of these. Which way of saying what I see I actually choose will depend on the particular circumstances of the case—for instance, on what sort of answer I expect you to be interested in, on how much I know, or on how far I am prepared to stick my neck out. (Nor is it a question of elongating my neck in a single dimension; it may be a planet, not a star, or Betelgeuse, not Sirius—but also, there may be only twelve mirrors in the telescope.)

'I saw an insignificant-looking man in black trousers.' 'I saw Hitler.' Two different senses of 'saw'? Of course not.

This fact—that we can normally describe, identify, or classify what we see in lots of different ways, sometimes differing in degree of adventurousness—not only makes it unnecessary and misguided to hunt up different senses of 'see'; it also shows incidentally that those philosophers are wrong who have held that the question, 'What do you see?' has only *one* right answer, for example, 'part of the surface of' whatever it may be. For if I can see part of the surface, for instance part of the top, of a table, of course I can also see, and can say that I see if in a position to do so, a table (a dining-table, a mahogany table, my bank-manager's table, &c.). This particular proposal has the further demerit that it would mean ruining the perfectly good word 'surface'; for not only is it wantonly wrong to say that what we see of a thing is always its *surface*; it is also wrong to imply that everything *has* a surface. Where and what exactly is the surface of a cat? Also, why 'part of'? If a piece of paper is laid before me in full view, it would be a wanton misuse to say that I see 'only part' of it, on the ground that I see (of course) only one side.

Another point which should at least be mentioned briefly is this. Although there is no good reason to say that 'perceive' ('see', &c.) have different *senses*, the fact that we can give different descriptions of what we perceive is certainly not the whole story. When something is seen, there may not only be different ways of *saying* what is seen; it may also be seen *in different ways*, seen *differently*. This possibility, which brings in the important formula 'see . . . *as* . . .', has been taken very seriously by psychologists, and also by Wittgenstein, but most philosophers who write about perception have scarcely noticed it. The clearest cases, no doubt, are those in which (as for instance with Wittgenstein's duck-rabbit) a picture or diagram is specially so devised as to be capable of being seen in different ways—as a duck or as a rabbit, as convex or concave, or whatever it may be. But the phenomenon also occurs, as one might say, naturally. A soldier will see the complex evolutions of men on a parade-ground differently from someone who knows nothing about drill; a painter, or at any rate a certain kind of painter, may well see a scene differently from someone unversed in the techniques of pictorial representation. Thus, different ways of saying what is seen will quite often be due, not just to differences in knowledge, in fineness of discrimination, in readiness to stick the neck out, or in interest in this aspect or that of the total situation; they may be due to the fact that what is seen is seen differently, seen in a different way, seen *as* this rather than that. And there will sometimes be no *one right* way of saying what is seen, for the additional reason that there may be no one right way of seeing it.[1] It is worth noticing that several of the examples we have come across in other contexts provide occasions for the use of the 'see . . . as' formula. Instead of saying that, to the naked eye, a distant star looks like a tiny speck, or appears as a tiny speck, we could say that it is *seen as* a tiny speck; instead

[1] Do we *normally* see things *as they really are*? Is this a fortunate fact, something that a psychologist might set about explaining? I should be inclined to resist the temptation to fall in with this way of speaking: 'seeing as' is for *special* cases. We sometimes say that we see a *person* 'as he really is'—'in his true colours'; but this is (*a*) an extended if not metaphorical use of 'see', (*b*) pretty well *confined* to the case of persons, and (*c*) a special case even within that limited field. Could it be said that we see, say, match-boxes in their true colours?

(3) seen as

of saying that, from the auditorium, the woman with her head in a black bag appears to be headless, or looks like a headless woman, we could say that she is *seen as* a headless woman.

But now we must turn back to the course of the philosophical argument. Ayer's section on 'the introduction of sense-data' consisted largely, you may remember, in attempts to establish the thesis that there are different 'senses'—two or perhaps more—of 'perceive' and other verbs of perception. I have argued that there is no reason at all to suppose that there are such different senses. Now it might be expected that this would be a serious matter for Ayer's argument; but curiously enough, I don't think it is. For though his argument is certainly presented *as if* it turned on this doctrine about different 'senses' of verbs of perception, it doesn't really turn on this doctrine at all.

The way in which sense-data are finally 'introduced', you remember, is this. Philosophers, it is said, decide to use 'perceive' ('see', &c.) in such a way 'that what is seen or otherwise sensibly experienced must really exist and must really have the properties that it appears to have'. This, of course, is not in fact the way in which 'perceive' ('see', &c.) is ordinarily used; nor, incidentally, is it any one of the ways of using these words which Ayer himself labels 'correct and familiar'; it is a *special* way of using these words, invented by philosophers. Well, having decided to use the words in this way, they naturally discover that, as candidates for what is perceived, 'material things' won't fill the bill; for material things don't always really have the properties they appear to have, and it may even seem that they exist when really they don't. Thus, though few philosophers if any are so brazen as to deny that material things are ever perceived in any 'sense' at all, at least something else has to be nominated as what is perceived in this special, philosophical sense. What is it that *does* fill the bill? And the answer is: sense-data.

Now the doctrine that there *already are*, in unphilosophical currency, different 'senses' of 'perceive' has as yet played no part in these manœuvres, which have consisted essentially in the invention of a quite *new* 'sense'. So what is its role? Well, according to Ayer (and Price), its role is that it provides the philosophers with the motive for inventing their own special sense.[1] Their own special sense is invented, according to Ayer, 'in order to avoid these ambiguities'. Now, the reason why it does not matter that no such ambiguities actually exist is that the avoidance of ambiguities is not in fact their motive. Their real motive—and this lies right at the heart of the whole matter—is that they wish to produce a species of statement that will be *incorrigible*; and the real virtue of this invented sense of 'perceive' is that, since what is perceived in this sense *has* to exist and *has* to be as it appears, in saying what I perceive in this sense I *can't be wrong*. All this must be looked into.

---

[1] To be quite accurate, Price regards the existence of these different 'senses' as a motive for inventing a special *terminology*. See *Perception*, p. 24: 'In this situation, the only safe course is to avoid the word "perceive" altogether.'

# X

THE PURSUIT OF THE INCORRIGIBLE IS ONE of the most venerable bugbears in the history of philosophy. It is rampant all over ancient philosophy, most conspicuously in Plato, was powerfully re-animated by Descartes, and bequeathed by him to a long line of successors. No doubt it has many motives and takes many forms, and naturally we can't go into the whole story now. In some cases the motive seems to be a comparatively simple hankering for something to be *absolutely certain*—a hankering which can be difficult enough to satisfy if one rigs it so that certainty is absolutely unattainable; in other cases, such as Plato's perhaps, what is apparently sought for is something that will be *always true*. But in the case now before us, which descends directly from Descartes, there is an added complication in the form of a general doctrine about knowledge. And it is of course knowledge, not perception at all, in which these philosophers are really interested. In Ayer's case this shows itself in the title of his book, as well as, *passim*, in his text; Price is more seriously interested than is Ayer in the actual facts about perception, and pays more attention to them—but still, it is worth noticing that, after raising the initial question, 'What is it to *see* something ?', his very next sentence runs,

'When I see a tomato there is much that I *can doubt*.'
This suggests that he too is really interested, not so much
in what seeing is, as in what one *can't* doubt.

In a nutshell, the doctrine about knowledge, 'empirical'
knowledge, is that it has *foundations*. It is a structure the
upper tiers of which are reached by inferences, and the
foundations are the *data* on which these inferences are
based. (So of course—as it appears—there just have to be
sense-data.) Now the trouble with inferences is that they
may be mistaken; whenever we take a step, we may put
a foot wrong. Thus—so the doctrine runs—the way to
identify the upper tiers of the structure of knowledge is
to ask whether one might be mistaken, whether there is
something that one *can doubt*; if the answer is Yes, then
one is not at the basement. And conversely, it will be
characteristic of the *data* that in their case no doubt is
possible, no mistake can be made. So to find the data, the
foundations, look for *the incorrigible*.

Now of course Ayer's exposition of this very old story
is (or at any rate was when it was written) very up-to-date,
very linguistic. He constantly reproves Price and his
other predecessors for treating as questions of fact what
are really questions of language. However, as we have
seen, this relative sophistication does not prevent Ayer
from swallowing whole almost all the old myths and
mistakes incorporated in the traditional arguments. Also,
as we have seen, it is not really true that he himself
believes the questions raised to be questions about language, though this is his official doctrine. And finally, as

we shall see in a moment, the doctrine that the questions *are* questions about language leads him, in the course of expounding it, to make about language a number of rather serious mistakes.

But before going into this, I should like to say one word more about this rift between Ayer's official views and his actual views. We detected it, earlier, in the second section of his book—to whit, in the startling conviction that there are no real facts about 'material things', we can say what we like about *them*, the only facts there really are are facts about 'phenomena', 'sensible appearances'. But the belief that really there *are* only sense-data emerges again, more clearly and much more frequently, in the final chapter, significantly entitled 'The Constitution of Material Things'. ('What are material things made of?') For example: 'As for the belief in the "unity" and "substantiality" of material things, I shall show that it may be correctly represented as involving no more than the attribution to visual and tactual sense-data of certain relations which do, *in fact*, obtain in our experience. And I shall show that it is only the contingent *fact that there are* these relations between sense-data that makes it *profitable to describe* the course of our experience in terms of the existence and behaviour of material things.' (The italics are mine.) Again: 'I can describe the task I am about to undertake as that of showing what are the general principles on which, *from our resources of sense-data*, we "construct" the world of material things.' Of course, the official interpretation of these and many other such

remarks is that, strictly speaking, they are concerned
with the logical relations obtaining between two different
*languages*, the 'sense-datum language' and 'material-
object language', and are not to be taken literally as concerned with the *existence* of anything. But it is *not* just
that Ayer sometimes speaks *as if* only sense-data in fact
existed, and *as if* 'material things' were really just jig-saw
constructions of sense-data. It is clear that he is actually
taking this to be true. For he holds without question that
empirical 'evidence' is supplied *only* by the occurrence of
sense-data, and that it is *for this reason* that 'any proposition that refers to a material thing *must somehow* be
expressible in terms of sense-data, if it is to be empirically significant'. (My italics again.) That is, the official
question, how these two supposed 'languages' may be
related to one another, is never regarded as genuinely
open; the material-object language *must somehow* be
'reducible' to the sense-datum language. Why? Because
in fact sense-data make up the whole of 'our resources'.

But we must go a bit further into this doctrine about
'two languages'. On this topic Ayer becomes involved in
a *fracas* with Carnap, and it will be instructive to see how
the argument between them goes.[1]

Carnap's doctrine on this subject, with which Ayer
finds himself in partial disagreement, is to the effect that
the (legitimate) indicative sentences of a language, other
than those which are analytic, can be divided into two

---

[1] Ayer, op. cit., pp. 84-92, 113-14.

groups, one group consisting of 'empirically testable' sentences, the other of 'observation-sentences', or 'protocols'. A sentence belongs to the first group, is empirically testable, if and only if, as Ayer puts it, some observation-sentence is 'derivable from it in accordance with the established rules of the language'. About these observation-sentences themselves Carnap has two things to say. He says (*a*) that it is fundamentally just a matter of convention which observation-sentences are taken to be *true*; all we need bother about is to fix it so that the total corpus of sentences we assert is internally consistent; and (*b*) that it doesn't much matter what sort of sentence we classify as an observation-sentence; for 'every concrete sentence belonging to the physicalistic system-language can in suitable circumstances serve as an observation-sentence'.

Now Ayer disagrees with Carnap on both of these points. On the first he argues, vehemently and perfectly correctly, that if anything we say is to have any serious claim to be in fact true (or even false) of the world we live in, then of course there have to be some things we say the truth (or falsehood) of which is determined by non-verbal reality; it can't be that everything we say has merely to be assessed for consistency with other things we say.

On the second point it is not *quite* so clear where Ayer stands. He holds—and this looks reasonable enough—that the only sentences which can properly be called 'observation-sentences' are those which record 'observable states of affairs'. But what kind of sentences do this? Or, as Ayer puts it, is it possible 'to delimit the class of propositions that are capable of being directly verified'? The trouble is that it is not quite clear how he answers this question. He begins by saying that 'it depends upon the language in which the proposition is expressed'. There is evidently no serious doubt that propositions about sense-data can be directly verified. 'On the other hand, when we are teaching English to a child, we imply that propositions about material things can be directly verified.' Well, perhaps we do; but are we right in implying this? Ayer sometimes seems to say that we can at any rate get away with it: but it is difficult to see how he could really think so. For (apart from his tendency, already noted, to express the conviction that the only real facts are facts about sense-data) there is the point that observation-sentences are regarded by him, as by Carnap, as the *termini* of processes of verification; and Ayer repeatedly expresses the view that propositions about 'material things' not only stand in need of verification themselves, but are actually incapable of being 'conclusively' verified. Thus, unless Ayer were prepared to say that propositions which *can't* be 'conclusively' verified *can* be 'directly' verified, and furthermore that they can figure as *termini* in processes of verification, he must surely deny that propositions about material things can be 'observation-sentences'. And in fact it is fairly clear, from the general trend of his argument as well as from its internal structure, that he does deny this. In the terms

used by Carnap, his real view seems to be that propositions about 'material things' are 'empirically testable',
propositions about sense-data are 'observation-sentences'; and whereas members of the first group are not
conclusively verifiable, members of the second group are
actually *incorrigible*.

We must now consider the rights and wrongs of all this.
Ayer is right, we have said already, and Carnap wrong, on
the question of connexion with non-verbal reality; the
idea that nothing at all comes in but the consistency of
sentences with each other is, indeed, perfectly wild. On
the second question, however, Carnap is at least more
nearly right than Ayer; there is indeed no special subclass of sentences whose business it is to count as evidence
for, or to be taken as verifying, other sentences, still less
whose special feature it is to be incorrigible. But Carnap
is not *quite* right even about this; for if we consider just
why he is nearly right, we shall see that the most important point of all here is one on which he and Ayer are
both equally mistaken.

Briefly, the point is this. It seems to be fairly generally
realized nowadays that, if you just take a bunch of sentences (or propositions,[1] to use the term Ayer prefers)

---

[1] The passage in which Ayer explains his use of this term (p. 102)
obscures *exactly* the essential point. For Ayer says (*a*) that in his use 'proposition' designates a class of sentences that all have *the same meaning*,
and (*b*) that 'consequently' he speaks of propositions, not sentences, as
being true or false. But of course to know what a sentence *means* does
*not* enable us to say that *it* is true or false; and that of which we can say
that it is true or false is *not* a 'proposition', in Ayer's sense.

impeccably formulated in some language or other, there
can be no question of sorting them out into those that are
true and those that are false; for (leaving out of account
so-called 'analytic' sentences) the question of truth and
falsehood does not turn only on what a sentence *is*, nor
yet on what it *means*, but on, speaking very broadly, the
circumstances in which it is uttered. Sentences are not
*as such* either true or false. But it is really equally clear,
when one comes to think of it, that for much the same
reasons there could be no question of picking out from
one's bunch of sentences those that are evidence for
others, those that are 'testable', or those that are 'incorrigible'. What kind of sentence is uttered as providing
evidence for what depends, again, on the circumstances
of particular cases; there is no kind of sentence which
*as such* is evidence-providing, just as there is no kind
of sentence which *as such* is surprising, or doubtful, or
certain, or incorrigible, or true. Thus, while Carnap is
quite right in saying that there is no special kind of sentence which *has* to be picked out as supplying the evidence for the rest, he is quite wrong in supposing that *any*
kind of sentence *could* be picked out in this way. It is not
that it doesn't much matter how we do it; there is really
no question of doing such a thing at all. And thus Ayer is
also wrong in holding, as he evidently does hold, that the
evidence-providing kind of sentences are always sense-
datum sentences, so that *these* are the ones that ought to be
picked out.

This idea that there is a certain kind, or form, of

sentence which as such is incorrigible and evidence-providing seems to be prevalent enough to deserve more detailed refutation. Let's consider incorrigibility first of all. The argument begins, it appears, from the observation that there are sentences which can be identified as intrinsically more adventurous than others, in uttering which we stick our necks out further. If for instance I say 'That's Sirius', I am wrong if, though it is a star, that star is not Sirius; whereas, if I had said only 'That's a star', its not being Sirius would leave me unshaken. Again, if I had said only, 'That looks like a star', I could have faced with comparative equanimity the revelation that it isn't a star. And so on. Reflections of this kind apparently give rise to the idea that there is or could be a kind of sentence in the utterance of which I take no chances *at all*, my commitment is absolutely minimal; so that in principle *nothing* could show that I had made a mistake, and my remark would be 'incorrigible'.

But in fact this ideal goal is completely unattainable. There isn't, there couldn't be, any kind of sentence which as such is incapable, once uttered, of being subsequently amended or retracted. Ayer himself, though he is prepared to say that sense-datum sentences are incorrigible, takes notice of one way in which they couldn't be; it is, as he admits, always possible in principle that, however non-committal a speaker intends to be, he may produce the *wrong word*, and subsequently be brought to admit this. But Ayer tries, as it were, to laugh this off as a quite trivial qualification; he evidently thinks that he is conceding here only the possibility of slips of the tongue, purely 'verbal' slips (or of course of lying). But this is not so. There are more ways than these of bringing out the wrong word. I may say 'Magenta' wrongly either by a mere slip, having meant to say 'Vermilion'; or because I don't know quite what 'magenta' means, what shade of colour is called *magenta*; or again, because I was unable to, or perhaps just didn't, really notice or attend to or properly size up the colour before me. Thus, there is always the possibility, not only that I may be brought to admit that 'magenta' wasn't the right word to pick on for the colour before me, but *also* that I may be brought to see, or perhaps remember, that the colour before me just wasn't *magenta*. And this holds for the case in which I say, 'It seems, to me personally, here and now, as if I were seeing something magenta', just as much as for the case in which I say, 'That is magenta.' The first formula may be more cautious, but it isn't *incorrigible*.[1]

[1] Ayer doesn't exactly *overlook* the possibility of misdescribing through inattention, failure to notice or to discriminate; in the case of sense-data he tries to *rule it out*. But this attempt is partly a failure, and partly unintelligible. To stipulate that a sense-datum has whatever qualities it appears to have is insufficient for the purpose, since it is *not* impossible to err even in saying only what qualities something appears to have—one may, for instance, not attend to its appearance carefully enough. But to stipulate that a sense-datum just is whatever the speaker takes it to be—so that if he *says* something different it must be a different sense-datum—amounts to making non-mendacious sense-datum statements true by *fiat*; and if so, how could sense-data be, as they are also meant to be, non-linguistic entities *of* which we are aware, *to* which we refer, that against which the factual truth of all empirical statements is ultimately to be tested?

Yes, but, it may be said, even if such cautious formulae
are not *intrinsically* incorrigible, surely there will be
plenty of cases in which what we say by their utterance
will *in fact* be incorrigible—cases in which, that is to say,
nothing whatever could actually be produced as a cogent
ground for retracting them. Well, yes, no doubt this is
true. But then exactly the same thing is true of utterances
in which quite different forms of words are employed.
For if, when I make some statement, it is true that nothing
whatever could in fact be produced as a cogent ground for
retracting it, this can only be because I am in, have got
myself into, the very best possible position for making
that statement—I have, and am entitled to have, *complete* confidence in it when I make it. But whether this
is so or not is not a matter of what *kind of sentence* I use
in making my statement, but of what *the circumstances
are* in which I make it. If I carefully scrutinize some patch
of colour in my visual field, take careful note of it, know
English well, and pay scrupulous attention to just what
I'm saying, I may say, 'It seems to me now as if I were
seeing something pink'; and nothing whatever could be
produced as showing that I had made a mistake. But
equally, if I watch for some time an animal a few feet in
front of me, in a good light, if I prod it perhaps, sniff, and
take note of the noises it makes, I may say, 'That's a pig';
and this too will be 'incorrigible', nothing could be produced that would show that I had made a mistake. Once
one drops the idea that there is a special *kind of sentence*
which is *as such* incorrigible, one might as well admit

(what is plainly true anyway) that *many* kinds of sentences may be uttered in making statements which are *in fact* incorrigible—in the sense that, when they are made, the circumstances are such that they are quite certainly, definitely, and un-retractably *true*.

Consider next the point about evidence—the idea that there is, again, some special kind of sentences whose function it is to formulate the evidence on which other kinds are based. There are at least two things wrong with this.

First, it is not the case, as this doctrine implies, that whenever a 'material-object' statement is made, the speaker must have or could produce evidence for it. This may sound plausible enough; but it involves a gross misuse of the notion of 'evidence'. The situation in which I would properly be said to have *evidence* for the statement that some animal is a pig is that, for example, in which the beast itself is not actually on view, but I can see plenty of pig-like marks on the ground outside its retreat. If I find a few buckets of pig-food, that's a bit more evidence, and the noises and the smell may provide better evidence still. But if the animal then emerges and stands there plainly in view, there is no longer any question of collecting evidence; its coming into view doesn't provide me with more *evidence* that it's a pig, I can now just *see* that it is, the question is settled. And of course I might, in different circumstances, have just seen this in the first place, and not had to bother with collecting evidence at all.[1] Again, if I actually see one man shoot

---

[1] I have, it will be said, the 'evidence of my own eyes'. But the point of

another, I may *give* evidence, as an eye-witness, to those less favourably placed; but I don't *have* evidence for my own statement that the shooting took place, I actually *saw* it. Once again, then, we find that you have to take into account, not just the words used, but the situation in which they are used; one who says 'It's a pig' will sometimes have evidence for saying so, sometimes not; one can't say that the *sentence* 'It's a pig', as such, is of a kind for which evidence is essentially required.

But secondly, as the case we've considered has already shown, it is not the case that the formulation of evidence is the function of any special sort of sentence. The evidence, if there is any, for a 'material-object' statement will usually be formulated in statements of just the same kind; but in general, *any* kind of statement could state evidence for *any* other kind, if the circumstances were appropriate. It is not true in general, for instance, that general statements are 'based on' singular statements and not vice versa; my belief that *this* animal will eat turnips may be based on the belief that most pigs eat turnips; though certainly, in different circumstances, I might have supported the claim that most pigs eat turnips by saying that this pig eats them at any rate. Similarly, and more relevantly perhaps to the topic of perception, it is not true in general that statements of how things are are 'based on' statements of how things appear, look, or seem and not vice versa. I may say, for instance, 'That pillar is

this trope is exactly that it does *not* illustrate the ordinary use of 'evidence'—that I *don't* have evidence in the ordinary sense.

bulgy' on the ground that it looks bulgy; but equally I might say, in different circumstances, 'That pillar looks bulgy'—on the ground that I've just built it, and I *built* it bulgy.

We are now in a position to deal quite briefly with the idea that 'material-object' statements are *as such* not conclusively verifiable. This is just as wrong as the idea that sense-datum statements are as such incorrigible (it is not just 'misleading', as Ayer is prepared to allow that it might be). Ayer's doctrine is that 'the notion of certainty does not apply to propositions *of this kind*'.[1] And his ground for saying this is that, in order to verify a proposition of this kind conclusively, we should have to perform the self-contradictory feat of completing 'an infinite series of verifications'; however many tests we may carry out with favourable results, we can never complete all the possible tests, for these are infinite in number; but nothing *less* than all the possible tests would be enough.

Now why does Ayer (and not he alone) put forward this very extraordinary doctrine? It is, of course, not true in general that statements about 'material things', as such, *need* to be 'verified'. If, for instance, someone remarks in casual conversation, 'As a matter of fact I live

---

[1] He is, incidentally, also wrong, as many others have been, in holding that the 'notion of certainty' *does* apply to 'the *a priori* propositions of logic and mathematics' as such. Many propositions in logic and mathematics are not certain at all; and if many are, that is not just because they *are* propositions in logic and mathematics, but because, say, they have been particularly firmly established.

in Oxford', the other party to the conversation may, if he finds it worth doing, verify this assertion; but the *speaker*, of course, has no need to do this—he knows it to be true (or, if he is lying, false). Strictly speaking, indeed, it is not just that he has no *need* to verify his statement; the case is rather that, since he already knows it to be true, nothing whatever that he might do could *count* as his 'verifying' it. Nor need it be true that he is in this position by virtue of having verified his assertion at some previous stage; for of how many people really, who know quite well where they live, could it be said that they have at any time *verified* that they live there? When could they be supposed to have done this? In what way? And why? What we have here, in fact, is an erroneous doctrine which is a kind of mirror-image of the erroneous doctrine about evidence we discussed just now; the idea that statements about 'material things' *as such* need to be verified is just as wrong as, and wrong in just the same way as, the idea that statements about 'material things' *as such* must be based on evidence. And both ideas go astray, at bottom, through the pervasive error of neglecting *the circumstances in which* things are said— of supposing that *the words alone* can be discussed, in a quite general way.

But even if we agree to confine ourselves to situations in which statements can be, and do need to be, verified, the case still looks desperate. Why on earth should one think that such verification can't ever be conclusive? If, for instance, you tell me there's a telephone in the next

*material things don't need verification*

room, and (feeling mistrustful) I decide to verify this, how could it be thought *impossible* for me to do this conclusively? I go into the next room, and certainly there's something there that looks exactly like a telephone. But is it a case perhaps of *trompe l'oeil* painting? I can soon settle that. Is it just a dummy perhaps, not really connected up and with no proper works? Well, I can take it to pieces a bit and find out, or actually use it for ringing somebody up—and perhaps get them to ring me up too, just to make sure. And of course, if I do all these things, I *do* make sure; what more could possibly be required? This object has already stood up to amply enough tests to establish that it really is a telephone; and it isn't just that, for everyday or practical or ordinary purposes, enough is *as good as* a telephone; what meets all these tests just *is* a telephone, no doubt about it.

However, as is only to be expected, Ayer has a reason for taking this extraordinary view. He holds, as a point of general doctrine, that, though in his view statements about 'material things' are never strictly equivalent to statements about sense-data, yet 'to say anything about a material thing is to say something, but not the same thing about classes of sense-data'; or, as he sometimes puts it, a statement about a 'material thing' *entails* 'some set of statements or other about sense-data'. But—and this is his difficulty—there is no *definite* and *finite* set of statements about sense-data entailed by any statement about a 'material thing'. Thus, however assiduously I check up on the sense-datum statements entailed by a statement about a 'material thing', I can never exclude the possibility that there are *other* sense-datum statements, which it also entails, but which, if checked, would turn out to be untrue. But of course, if a statement may be found to entail a false statement, then it itself may thereby be found to be false; and this is a possibility which, according to the doctrine, cannot in principle be finally eliminated. And since, again according to the doctrine, verification just consists in thus checking sense-datum statements, it follows that verification can *never* be conclusive.[1]

Of the many objectionable elements in this doctrine, in some ways the strangest is the use made of the notion of entailment. What does the sentence, 'That is a pig', *entail*? Well, perhaps there is somewhere, recorded by some zoological authority, a statement of the necessary and sufficient conditions for belonging to the species *pig*. And so perhaps, if we use the word 'pig' strictly in that sense, to say of an animal that it's a pig will entail that it satisfies those conditions, whatever they may be. But clearly it isn't this sort of entailment that Ayer has in mind; nor, for that matter, is it particularly relevant to the use that non-experts make of the word 'pig'.[2] But what other kind of entailment is there? We have a pretty rough idea what pigs look like, what they smell and sound

[1] Material things are put together like jig-saw puzzles; but since the number of pieces in a puzzle is not finite, we can never know that any puzzle is perfect, there may be pieces missing or pieces that won't fit.

[2] Anyway, the official definition won't cover *everything*—freaks, for instance. If I'm shown a five-legged pig at a fair, I can't get my money back on the plea that being a pig entails having only four legs.

like, and how they normally behave; and no doubt, if
something didn't look at all right for a pig, behave as pigs
do, or make pig-like noises and smells, we'd say that it
wasn't a pig. But are there—do there *have* to be—*statements* of the form, 'It looks ...', 'It sounds ...', 'It
smells ...', of which we could say straight off that 'That
is a pig' entails them? Plainly not. We learn the word
'pig', as we learn the vast majority of words for ordinary
things, ostensively—by being told, in the presence of the
animal, '*That* is a pig'; and thus, though certainly we
learn what sort of thing it is to which the word 'pig' can
and can't be properly applied, we don't go through any
kind of intermediate stage of relating the word 'pig' to a
lot of *statements* about the way things look, or sound, or
smell. The word is just not introduced into our vocabulary in this way. Thus, though of course we come to
have certain expectations as to what will and won't be
the case when a pig is in the offing, it is wholly artificial
to represent these expectations in the guise of *statements
entailed by* 'That is a pig.' And for just this reason it is, at
best, wholly artificial to speak as if *verifying* that some
animal is a pig consists in checking up on the statements
entailed by 'That is a pig.' If we do think of verification
in this way, certainly difficulties abound; we don't know
quite where to begin, how to go on, or where to stop. But
what this shows is, not that 'That is a pig' is very difficult
to verify or incapable of being conclusively verified, but
that this is an impossible travesty of verification. If the
procedure of verification were rightly described in this

way, then indeed we couldn't say just what would constitute conclusive verification that some animal was a pig.
But this doesn't show that there is actually any difficulty
at all, usually, in verifying that an animal is a pig, if we
have occasion to do so; it shows only that what verification *is* has been completely misrepresented.[1]

We may add to this the rather different but related
point that, though certainly we have more or less definite
views as to what objects of particular kinds will and
won't do, and of how they will and won't re-act in one
situation or another, it would again be grossly artificial
to represent these in the guise of definite entailments.
There are vast numbers of things which I take it for
granted that a telephone won't do, and doubtless an infinite number of things which it never enters my head to
consider the possibility that it might do; but surely it
would be perfectly absurd to say that 'This is a telephone'
*entails* the whole galaxy of statements to the effect that
it doesn't and won't do these things, and to conclude that
I haven't *really* established that anything is a telephone
until, *per impossibile*, I have confirmed the whole infinite

---

[1] Another way of showing that 'entailment' is out of place in such contexts: Suppose that tits, all the tits we've ever come across, are bearded,
so that we are happy to say 'Tits are bearded.' Does this *entail* that what
isn't bearded isn't a tit? Not really. For if beardless specimens are discovered in some newly explored territory, well, of course we weren't
talking about *them* when we said that tits were bearded; we now have to
think again, and recognize perhaps this new species of glabrous tits.
Similarly, what we say nowadays about tits just doesn't refer *at all* to the
prehistoric eo-tit, or to remote future tits, defeathered perhaps through
some change of atmosphere.

class of these supposed entailments. Does 'This is a telephone' *entail* 'You couldn't eat it'? Must I try to eat it, and fail, in the course of making sure that it's a telephone?[1]

The conclusions we have reached so far, then, can be summed up as follows:

1. There is no *kind* or *class* of sentences ('propositions') of which it can be said that *as such*

(*a*) they are incorrigible;
(*b*) they provide the evidence for other sentences; and
(*c*) they must be checked in order that other sentences may be verified.

2. It is not true of sentences about 'material things' that *as such*

(*a*) they must be supported by or based on evidence;
(*b*) they stand in need of verification; and
(*c*) they cannot be conclusively verified.

Sentences in fact—as distinct from *statements made in particular circumstances*—cannot be divided up *at all* on these principles, into two groups or any other number of groups. And this means that the general doctrine about

---

[1] Philosophers, I think, have taken too little notice of the fact that most words in ordinary use are defined ostensively. For example, it has often been thought to be a puzzle why A *can't* be B, if being A doesn't *entail* being not-B. But it is often just that 'A' and 'B' are brought in as ostensively defined as, words for *different things*. Why can't a Jack of Hearts be a Queen of Spades? Perhaps we need a new term, 'ostensively analytic'.

knowledge which I sketched at the beginning of this section, which is the real bugbear underlying doctrines of
the kind we have been discussing, is *radically* and *in
principle* misconceived. For even if we were to make the
very risky and gratuitous assumption that what some
particular person knows at some particular place and
time could systematically be sorted out into an arrangement of foundations and super-structure, it would be a
mistake in principle to suppose that the same thing could
be done for knowledge *in general*. And this is because
there *could* be no *general* answer to the questions what is
evidence for what, what is certain, what is doubtful, what
needs or does not need evidence, can or can't be verified.
If the Theory of Knowledge consists in finding grounds
for such an answer, there is no such thing.

Before leaving this topic, though, there is one more
doctrine about the 'two languages' that we ought to consider. This final doctrine is wrong for reasons not quite
the same as those we have just been discussing, and it has
a certain interest in its own right.

It is not very easy to say just what the doctrine is, so
I shall give it in Ayer's own words (with my italics). He
says for instance: 'Whereas the meaning of a sentence
which refers to a sense-datum is *precisely determined* by
the rule that correlates it with the sense-datum in question, such *precision* is not attainable in the case of a sentence which refers to a material thing. For the proposition
which such a sentence expresses differs from a proposition
about a sense-datum in that there are no observable facts

that constitute both a necessary and sufficient condition of its truth.'[1] And again: '. . . one's references to material things are *vague* in their application to phenomena . . . .'[2] Well, perhaps it isn't very clear just what is meant by these remarks; still, it is clear enough that what is being said is that statements about sense-data—all such statements—are, in some way or in some sense, *precise*, while by contrast statements about material things are—*all* are —*vague* in some sense or some way. It is, for a start, difficult to see how this could be true. Is 'Here are three pigs' a vague statement? Is 'It seems to me as if I were seeing something sort of pinkish' *not* vague? Is the second statement *necessarily* precise in a way in which the first just couldn't be? And isn't it surprising that precision should be paired off with *incorrigibility*, vagueness with *impossibility of verification*? After all we speak of people 'taking refuge' in vagueness—the more precise you are, in general the more likely you are to be wrong, whereas you stand a good chance of *not* being wrong if you make it vague enough. But what we really need to do here is to take a closer look at 'vague' and 'precise' themselves.

'Vague' is itself vague. Suppose that I say that something, for instance somebody's description of a house, is vague; there is a quite large number of possible features— not necessarily defects, that depends on what is wanted— any or all of which the description might have and which

---

[1] Ayer, op. cit., p. 110. 'Observable facts' here, as so often, means, and can only mean, 'facts about sense-data'.

[2] Ayer, op. cit., p. 242.

might lead me to pronounce it vague. It might be (*a*) a *rough* description, conveying only a 'rough idea' of the thing to be described; or (*b*) *ambiguous* at certain points, so that the description would fit, might be taken to mean, either this or that; or (*c*) *imprecise*, not precisely specifying the features of the thing described; or (*d*) not very *detailed*; or (*e*) couched in *general terms* that would cover a lot of rather different cases; or (*f*) not very *accurate*; or perhaps also (*g*) not very *full*, or *complete*. A description might, no doubt, exhibit all these features at once, but clearly they can also occur independently of each other. A rather rough and incomplete description may be quite accurate as far as it goes; it may be detailed but very imprecise, or quite unambiguous but still very general. In any case, it is clear enough that there is not just *one* way of being vague, or one way of being not vague, viz. being *precise*.

Usually it is *uses* of words, not words themselves, that are properly called 'vague'. If, for instance, in describing a house, I say among other things that it has a roof, my not saying what kind of roof it has may be one of the features which lead people to say that my description is a bit vague; but there seems no good reason why the word 'roof' itself should be said to be a vague *word*. Admittedly there are different kinds of roofs, as there are different kinds of pigs and policemen; but this does not mean that all uses of 'roof' are such as to leave us in some doubt as to just what is meant; sometimes we may wish the speaker to be 'more precise', but for this there would presumably be some special reason. This feature of being applicable over a considerable range of non-identical instances is, of course, enormously common; far more words exhibit it than, I think, we should want to label as, in general, vague *words*. Again, almost any word may land us in difficulty over marginal cases; but this again is not enough to make a charge of vagueness stick. (Incidentally the reason why many words exhibit these features is not that they occur in 'material-object' language, but that they occur in *ordinary* language, where excessive nicety of distinction would be positively tiresome; they stand in contrast, not with 'sense-datum' words, but with the special terminologies of the 'exact sciences'.) There are, however, a few notoriously useless words—'democracy', for instance—uses of which are always liable to leave us in real doubt what is meant; and here it seems reasonable enough to say that the *word* is vague.

The classic stamping-ground of 'precise' is the field of *measurement*; here, being precise is a matter of using a sufficiently finely graduated scale. '709·864 feet' is a very precise answer to the question how long the liner is (though it might not be accurate). *Words* may be said to be precise when, as one may put it, their application is fixed within narrow limits; 'duck-egg blue' is at least a *more* precise term than 'blue'. But there is, of course, no general answer to the question how finely graduated a scale must be, or how narrowly determined the application of a word, for precision to be achieved—partly because there is no terminus to the business of making ever finer divisions and discriminations, and partly because what is precise (enough) for some purposes will be much too rough and crude for others. A description, for example, can no more be absolutely, finally, and ultimately *precise* than it can be absolutely *full* or *complete*.

'Precisely' can be, and should be, distinguished from 'exactly'. If I measure a banana with a ruler, I may find it to be precisely 5⅝ inches long. If I measure my ruler with bananas, I may find it to be exactly six bananas long, though I couldn't claim any great precision for my method of measurement. If I have to divide a load of sand into three equal parts, having no means of weighing it, I can't do it *precisely*. But if I have to divide a pile of 26 bricks into three equal piles, I can't do it *exactly*. One might say there is something exciting, specially noteworthy, where 'exactly' is used—its being *exactly* two o'clock has, so to speak, better news-value than its being three minutes past; and there's a kind of exhilaration in finding the *exact word* (which may not be a precise word).

Then what about 'accurate'? Plainly enough, neither a word nor a sentence can, as such, be accurate. Consider maps, for instance, where accuracy is most comfortably at home; an accurate map is not, so to speak, a *kind* of map, as for instance is a large-scale, a detailed, or a clearly drawn map—its accuracy is a matter of the *fit* of the map *to* the terrain it is a map of. One is tempted to say that an accurate report, for instance, must be *true* whereas a very precise or detailed report may not be; and there is something right in this idea, though I feel rather uneasy about it. Certainly 'untrue but accurate' is pretty clearly wrong; but 'accurate and therefore true' doesn't seem quite right either. Is it only that 'true', after 'accurate', is redundant? It would be worth while to compare here the relation of 'true' to, say, 'exaggerated'; if 'exaggerated and *therefore* untrue' seems not quite right, one might try 'untrue *in the sense that* it's exaggerated', 'untrue, *or rather*, exaggerated', or '*to the extent that* it's exaggerated, untrue'. Of course, just as no word or phrase is accurate as such, no word or phrase is as such an exaggeration. Here, though, we are digressing.

What are we to make, then, of the idea that sentences about sense-data are as such precise, while sentences about 'material things' are intrinsically vague? The second part of this doctrine is intelligible, in a way. What Ayer seems to have in mind is that being a cricket-ball, for instance, does not entail being looked at rather than felt, looked at in any special light or from any particular distance or angle, felt with the hand rather than the foot, &c. . . . This of course is perfectly true; and the only comment required is that it constitutes no ground at all for saying that 'That is a cricket-ball' is vague. Why should we say that it is vague 'in its application to phenomena'? The expression is surely not meant to 'apply to phenomena'. It is meant to identify a particular kind of ball—a kind which is, in fact, quite *precisely* defined— and this it does perfectly satisfactorily. What would the speaker make of a request to be *more* precise? Incidentally, as has been pointed out before, it would be a mistake to assume that greater precision is always an improvement; for it is, in general, more difficult to be more precise; and the more precise a vocabulary is, the less easily adaptable it is to the demands of novel situations.

But the first part of the doctrine is much less easy to understand. By saying that 'the meaning of a sentence which refers to a sense-datum is precisely determined by the rule that correlates it with *the sense-datum* in question', Ayer can hardly mean that such a sentence can refer only to *one particular* sense-datum; for if this were so there could be no sense-datum *language* (but only, I suppose, 'sense-datum names'). On the other hand, why on earth should it be true *in general* that expressions used in referring to sense-data should be precise? A difficulty here is that it is never really made clear whether Ayer regards the 'sense-datum language' as something which already exists and which we use, or whether he thinks of it as a merely possible language which could in principle be invented; for this reason one never knows quite what one is supposed to be considering, or where to look for examples. But this scarcely matters for the present purpose; whether we are to think of an existent or an artificial language, there is in any case no necessary connexion between reference to sense-data and *precision*; the classificatory terms to be used might be extremely rough and general, why ever not? It is true presumably that reference to sense-data couldn't be 'vague in its application to phenomena' in *just* the way Ayer holds that reference to 'material things' *must* be; but then this isn't really a way of being vague. And even if it had been, it is still pretty obvious that avoidance of it would not guarantee precision. There are more ways of being vague than one.

Thus, to the summary we set out a few pages ago we can now add this: there is no reason to say that expressions used in referring to 'material things' are (as such, intrinsically) vague; and there is no reason to suppose that expressions used in referring to 'sense-data' would be (as such, necessarily) precise.

# XI

I CONCLUDE WITH SOME REMARKS ON PART of Warnock's book on Berkeley.[1] In this book, with much of which I am in general agreement, Warnock shows himself to be a relatively wary practitioner; and of course he was writing a great many years later than were Price and Ayer. All the same, I think it is clear that something goes badly wrong; for he ends up with a dichotomy between two kinds of statements, one about 'ideas' and the other about 'material objects', of just the kind which I have been arguing against all along. Admittedly what Warnock is trying to do is to produce a version of Berkeley's doctrine, removing what he regards as unnecessary mistakes and obscurities; he is not, that is, explicitly setting out views of his own. Still, some views of his own do emerge in the course of the discussion; and in any case I shall argue that he regards his version of Berkeley's doctrines with far too indulgent an eye. It all runs quite smoothly, there's positively no deception: and yet in the end that baby has somehow been spirited down the waste-pipe.

Warnock begins (in the passage we're concerned with) by undertaking to explain what Berkeley meant, or at least what he should have meant, by the dictum that only 'our

[1] Warnock, *Berkeley*, chapters 7–9.

own ideas' are 'immediately perceived'. Why, to begin
with, did Berkeley raise an objection to such everyday
remarks as that we see chairs and rainbows, hear coaches
and voices, smell flowers and cheese? It is not, Warnock
says, that he regarded such remarks as never *true*; his
notion was that in saying such things we are speaking
*loosely*.[1] Although there is no great harm in saying, for
instance, that I hear a coach on the road, 'strictly speaking, what I actually *hear* is a sound'. And similarly in
other cases; our ordinary judgements of perception are
always 'loose', in the sense that they go beyond what we
actually perceive, we make 'inferences' or assumptions.

Warnock's comment on this is that we commonly do,
as Berkeley says, make assumptions and take things for
granted in saying what (for instance) we see; however,
he thinks that Berkeley is wrong in holding that to do
this is always to speak loosely. 'For in order to report
correctly what I actually see, it is sufficient for me to
confine my statement to what, on the basis of sight on
the present occasion, I am *entitled to say*; and in good
conditions of observation, I am certainly entitled to say
that I see a book'; and again, 'to make no assumptions
about what makes the noises that I hear is to be specially

[1] In fact Warnock leaves Berkeley's point in considerable obscurity, by
purporting to state it in a bewildering variety of ways. Besides saying that
Berkeley is against speaking 'loosely', he also represents him from time
to time as in pursuit of *accuracy*, *precision*, *strictness*, and *clarity*; of the
*correct* use of words, the *proper* use of words; of the use of words that *fit*
the facts *closely*, that express no more than we are *entitled to say*. He
seems to regard all of these as somehow much the same.

cautious in saying what I hear; but correct speech does not require us always to be as cautious as possible'. It is true, Warnock thinks, that the question, 'What did you actually see?' requires the answerer to be *less* liberal with his assumptions, extraneous evidence, &c., than does the question, 'What did you see?'; but it does not demand that they should be eliminated altogether, and Berkeley is wrong in suggesting that, 'strictly', this is necessary.

On at least one point, though, Warnock himself has gone astray here. He illustrates the distinction between 'see' and 'actually see' by the case of a witness under cross-examination, who is sharply instructed to confine his remarks to what he *actually saw*; and he concludes from this (one!) example that to say what one actually saw is always to draw in one's horns a bit, to be a bit more cautious, to reduce the claim. But this just isn't true in general; it may be just the other way round. I might begin, for instance, by saying that I saw a little silvery speck, and go on to say that what I actually saw was a star. I might say in evidence that I saw a man firing a gun, and say afterwards, 'I actually saw him committing the murder!' That is (to put it shortly and roughly), sometimes I may supposedly see, or take it that I see, *more* than I actually see, but sometimes *less*. Warnock is hypnotized by the case of the nervous witness. Before resting any weight on this word 'actually', he would have been well advised not only to consider a lot more examples of its use, but also to compare it with such related phrases as 'really', 'in fact', 'in actual fact', 'as a matter of fact'.

But in any case, Warnock continues, Berkeley is really concerned not with the question what we *actually* perceive, but with his own question, what we *immediately* perceive. About this he says that 'the expression has no ordinary use at all', so that Berkeley is perfectly entitled, he thinks, to use it in any way he likes. (This in itself is decidedly over-bold. 'Immediately perceive' may not have a *clear* meaning; but 'immediately' at any rate is quite an ordinary word, of which the ordinary meaning certainly does have implications and associations on which, as a matter of fact, the argument trades very substantially.) Well, how does Berkeley use this expression? Warnock explains as follows: 'I say, for instance, that I see a book. Let it be admitted that this is a perfectly correct thing to say. But there is still in this situation something (not the book) which is *immediately* seen. For, whether or not any further investigations would confirm the claim that I see a book, whatever I know or believe about what I see, and whatever I might see, touch, or smell if I came closer, there is *now* in my visual field a certain coloured shape, or pattern of colours. This is what I *immediately* see. . . . This is more "fundamental" than the book itself, in the sense that, although I might immediately see this pattern of colours and yet no book be there, I could not see the book nor indeed *anything at all* unless such coloured shapes occurred in my visual field.'

But *does* this introduce the expression 'immediately perceive' satisfactorily? It seems that what I am to be said to see 'immediately' must be what is 'in my visual field'. But this latter phrase is not explained at all; isn't the book in my visual field? And if the right answer to the question what is in my visual field is to be, as Warnock assumes, 'a coloured shape', why should one further assume that this is 'something, *not the book*'? It would surely be quite natural and proper to say, 'That patch of red there *is* the book' (cp. 'That white dot is my house'). By ignoring the fact that coloured shapes, patches of colour, &c. can quite often and correctly be said to *be* the things that we see, Warnock is just quietly slipping in here that dichotomy between 'material objects' and entities of some other kind which is so crucially damaging. Furthermore, he has himself admitted in several earlier passages that patches of colour, &c. can be and are said to be seen in a perfectly ordinary, familiar sense; so why do we now have to say that they are *immediately* seen, as if they called for some special treatment?

Warnock's exposition next takes quite a new turn. So far, he seems to have been falling in with Berkeley's views to the extent of conceding that there are *entities* of some sort—not 'material things'—which are what we 'immediately perceive'. But in the next two chapters he takes the linguistic line, attempting to distinguish the *kind of sentence* which expresses a 'judgement of immediate perception'. Starting from Berkeley's dictum that 'the senses make no inferences', Warnock sets off on the familiar process of refining down and cutting away, with the intention of arriving at the ideally basic, completely minimal form of assertion. He gets off to rather a bad start, however, which reveals him as already at least half-way to perdition. What he is looking for, he says, is a kind of assertion 'in the making of which we "make no inferences"', or (as we have suggested it would be better to say) take nothing for granted, make no assumptions'. From the way he puts it, it is clear that he is making the (by now) familiar mistake of supposing that there is some special *form of words* that will meet this requirement, while other forms of words do not. But his own examples serve to show that this *is* a mistake. Consider, he says, the statement, 'I hear a car'. This is non-minimal, he says, not a statement of 'immediate perception', since, when I make this judgement, the sound that I hear leads me 'to make certain assumptions, which further investigation might show to have been mistaken'. But in fact the question whether I am making assumptions which might turn out to be mistaken depends, not on the form of words I use, but on the circumstances in which I am placed. The situation Warnock evidently has in mind is that in which I hear a car-like sound, but have nothing *except* this sound to go on. But what if I already know that there is a car just outside? What if I can actually see it, and perhaps touch and smell it as well? What would I *then* be 'assuming', if I were to say, 'I hear a car'? What 'further investigation' would be necessary, or even possible?[1] To make the form of words 'I hear a car' look

---

[1] Part of the trouble is that Warnock never makes clear enough just *what* is supposed to be assumed, or taken for granted. Sometimes he

*intrinsically* vulnerable, by implying that their utterance *can only* be based on just hearing a sound, is little better than a frame-up.

Again, Warnock condemns as also non-minimal the form of words 'I hear a sort of purring noise', on the ground that one who says this is assuming that he isn't wearing ear-plugs; it might really be a very loud noise, which just sounds purring to him, because of the ear-plugs. But one can't seriously say to someone, 'But you might be wearing ear-plugs' *whenever* he utters that form of words; he isn't necessarily *assuming* that he isn't, he may *know* that he isn't, and the suggestion that he might be may itself be perfectly absurd. Although Warnock insists that neither he nor Berkeley has any intention of casting doubt on the judgements we ordinarily make, of arguing for any brand of philosophical scepticism, this procedure of representing forms of words as *in general* vulnerable is, of course, one of the major devices by which sceptical theses have commonly been insinuated. To say, as Warnock does, that we are making assumptions and taking things for granted *whenever* we make an ordinary assertion, is of course to make ordinary assertions look somehow chancy, and it's no good his saying that he and Berkeley don't mean to do that. One might add that Warnock subtly intensifies this air of chanciness by taking his examples from the sphere of hearing. It is, as

seems to have in mind further facts about the present situation, sometimes the outcome of future investigations by the speaker, sometimes the question of what other observers would report. But can it be assumed that these all come to much the same?

a matter of fact, quite often true that, just going by the sound, we do make some sort of inference in saying what we hear, and it is quite often easy to see how we might go wrong. But then seeing is *not*, as Warnock quietly takes for granted, exactly like this; for it is, characteristically, by seeing the thing that the question is settled.

What Warnock is really trying to do, though, is to produce, not a maximally certain, but a *minimally adventurous* form of words, by the use of which we can always stick our necks out as little as possible. And in the end he arrives at the formula, 'It seems to me now as if . . .' as the general prefix which guarantees 'immediacy', keeps the speaker within the bounds of 'his own ideas'. Berkeley's doctrine that material objects are 'collections of ideas' can then be presented, Warnock thinks, in linguistic dress, as the doctrine that a sentence about a material object *means the same as* an indefinitely large collection of appropriate sentences beginning, 'It seems to . . . as if . . . .' 'Any statement about any material thing is really (can be analysed into) an indefinitely large set of statements about what it seems, or in suitable conditions would seem, as if the speaker and other people and God were hearing, seeing, feeling, tasting, smelling.'

Now Warnock, rightly enough, finds this version of the relation between statements about 'material things' and statements about 'ideas' unacceptable. There is indeed something absurd in the idea that all we can ever really do is to pile up more and more statements as to how things seem; and if this is what Berkeley meant, then the people who said he failed to do justice to 'the reality of things' had right on their side. But Warnock doesn't leave it at that; he goes on to say that statements about 'material things' are not *the same* as sets of statements about how things seem—the two kinds of statements are related as *verdicts* to *evidence*, or at least the relation, he says, is 'very similar'. 'There is an essential logical difference between discussing evidence and pronouncing verdicts—a difference which cannot be abolished by any amount, however vast, of piling up evidence, however conclusive. . . . Similarly, there is an essential logical difference between saying how things seem and how they are—a difference which cannot be removed by assembling more and more reports of how things seem.'

But this comparison is really quite disastrous. It clearly involves falling in with a number of the mistakes we mentioned earlier on—with the idea, for instance, that statements about 'material things' *as such* are always, have to be, based on evidence, and that there is a particular other kind of sentence the business of which is to be evidence-providing. But, as we saw, whether or not I have, or need, *evidence* for what I say is not a question of the kind of sentence I utter, but of the circumstances in which I am placed; and if evidence is produced or needed, there is no special kind of sentence, no form of words, by which this has to be done.

But Warnock's comparison also leads directly to just the kind of 'scepticism' which he is officially anxious to disavow. For verdicts are given, in the light of the evidence, by judges or juries—that is to say, precisely by people who were *not* actual *witnesses* of the matter in question. To give a verdict on evidence is precisely to pronounce on some matter on which one is not a first-hand authority. So to say that statements about 'material things' are in general like verdicts is to imply that we are never, that we can't be, in the best position to make them—that, so to speak, there is no such thing as being an eye-witness of what goes on in the 'material world', we can only get evidence. But to put the case in this way is to make it seem quite reasonable to suggest that we can never *know*, we can never be *certain*, of the truth of anything we say about 'material things'; for after all, it appears, we have nothing but the evidence to go on, we have no direct access to what is really going on, and verdicts of course are notoriously fallible. But how absurd it is, really, to suggest that I am *giving a verdict* when I say what is going on under my own nose! It is just this kind of comparison which does the real damage.

Furthermore, Warnock's picture of the situation gets it upside-down as well as distorted. His statements of 'immediate perception', so far from being that from which we *advance* to more ordinary statements, are actually arrived at, and are so arrived at in his own account, by *retreating from* more ordinary statements, by progressive hedging. (There's a tiger—there *seems* to be a tiger—it seems *to me* that there's a tiger—it seems to me *now* that there's a tiger—it seems to me now *as if there were* a tiger.) It seems extraordinarily perverse to represent as that on which ordinary statements are based a form of words which, *starting from* and moreover incorporating an ordinary statement, qualifies and hedges it in various ways. You've got to get something on your plate before you can start messing it around. It is not, as Warnock's language suggests, that we can stop hedging if there is a good case for coming right out with it; the fact is that we don't *begin* to hedge unless there is some special reason for doing so, something a bit strange and off-colour about the particular situation.

But what is generally, and most importantly, wrong with Warnock's argument is simply that he has got into (perhaps has let Berkeley lead him into) the position of swallowing the two-languages doctrine—temporarily, at least, appearing to swallow the two-entities doctrine on the way. And the resulting question about how the evidence-language ('idea'-language) is related to material-object-language, which he tries to answer, is a question that *has* no answer, it's a quite unreal question. The main thing is not to get bamboozled into asking it at all. Warnock, I think, makes matters even worse by hitting on the particular formula, 'It seems as if . . .'; for this formula is already heavily loaded with the ideas of passing judgement, assessing evidence, reaching tentative verdicts. But nothing else would be much better as a limb of this quite bogus dichotomy. The right policy is not the one that Warnock adopts, of trying to patch it up a bit and make it work properly; that just can't be done. The right policy is to go back to a much earlier stage, and to dismantle the whole doctrine before it gets off the ground.

# INDEX

'Accurate', 128-9.
'Actually', 134-5.
Appearance, and reality, Ayer's account of, 78-83.
Appearances, visual, 21, 30.
'Appears', 35, 36-38.
Aristotle, 64, 70 n.
Ayer, A. J., 1, 6, 8, 19, 33, 124, 125 n., 129-30, 132.
— on appearance and reality, 78-83.
— on argument from illusion, 20-22, 25, 28-32, 55-61.
— on corrigibility and verification, 104-13, 117, 119.
— on sense-data, 44-48, 50-54, 84-98, 102, 103.

Berkeley, 1, 4, 61, 132-6, 138, 139, 142.

Carnap, R., 107-11.
Certainty, 10, 104, 117.
Colour, 'real', 65-66, 82-83.
— patches of, 136.

Deception, by the senses, 8, 9, 11-14, 52.
Definition, ostensive, 121, 122 n.
Delusion, distinguished from illusion, 20-25; see also Perceptions.
Descartes, 1, 11, 49 n., 104.
Dreams, 12, 27, 42, 48-49.

Entailment, 119-23.
Evidence, 111, 115-17, 123, 140-2.

'Exact', 128.
'Exist', 68 n.

Facts, empirical, Ayer's view of, 59-61, 84, 87, 106-7, 124.
Field, visual, 136.
Freaks, 120 n.

Ghosts, 14, 24, 95 n.
'Good', 64, 69-70, 73, 76 n.

Hallucination, 20, 67, 69.
Heraclitus, 1.
Hume, 4, 61.

Incorrigibility, 42, 103, 110-15, 123, 125.
Illusion, argument from, 4, 19, 20-32, 33, 44-54, 55-61.
— argument from, Ayer's evaluation of, 55-61.
— distinguished from delusion 22-25.
— Price's definition of, 27-28.

Kant, 61.
Knowledge, theory of, 104-5, 124.

Language, ordinary, 62-64.
— ordinary, Ayer's view of, 55-56, 109.
'Like', 41-42, 74-76.
Locke, 6, 10, 61.
'Looks', 34, 36-43.

Manifold, sensible, 61.
Material-object language, 107, 127, 142.

Measurement, 127–8.
Mirages, 21, 24–25, 32.
Mirror-images, 12, 20, 26, 31, 50.

Naïve Realism, 9 n.

Observation-sentences, 108–10.

Perception, direct and indirect, 2, 7, 10, 15–19, 29, 44, 87.
— immediate, 133–7, 141.
— verbs of, different senses of, 85–103.
Perceptions, delusive and veridical, 44–54, 55, 86–87.
— existentially and qualitatively delusive, 78–83.
Perspective, 12, 20, 26, 28.
Pitcher, G. W., viii.
Plato, 2, 104.
'Precise', 124, 126, 127–8, 129–31.
Price, H. H., 1, 8 n., 9 n., 27, 28, 45–48, 50, 52, 61, 86 n., 103–5, 132.
Processes, cerebral, 45, 51, 64.
Propositions, Ayer's account of, 110 n.
Protocols, 108.

'Real', 15 n., 59, 62–67, 78, 80–83; *see also* Appearance.
— as 'adjuster-word', 73–76.
— as 'dimension-word', 71–73.
— as 'substantive-hungry', 68–70.
— as 'trouser-word', 70–71.
Realism, 3.
Refraction, 20, 21, 25, 26, 51.
Russell, Earl, 4.

Scepticism, 138, 140.
Scholasticism, 3, 4, 13.
'Seeing as', 92, 100–2.
'Seems', 36, 37–39, 43, 142.
Sense-data, 2, 7, 8, 55–57, 60–61, 80, 81, 105–7, 109, 113 n., 119–20, 129–31.
— as directly perceived, 44–54.
— as objects of delusive experiences, 20–22, 27–32.
— Ayer's introduction of, 84–87, 102–3.
Sense-datum language, 107, 130.
Sense-perceptions, 6, 11.
Senses, testimony of the, 11.
Sentences, empirically testable, 108–10.
— distinguished from statements, 110–11, 123.
Surfaces, 27–28, 100.

Thales, 4.

Universals, 2, 4 n.
Urmson, J. O., ix.

'Vague', 125–7, 129–31.
Verdicts, 140–2.
'Veridical', 11, 22; *see also* Perceptions.
Verification, direct, 109.
— conclusive, 109, 117–23.
Vision, double, 20, 85, 89–92, 97.

Warnock, G. J., 1, 132–42.
Wittgenstein, 100.

# GALAXY BOOKS

| | | |
|---|---|---|
| Aaron, Daniel | *Men of Good Hope* | GB58 |
| Abrams, Meyer H., ed. | *English Romantic Poets* | GB35 |
| Agarwala and Singh, eds. | *The Economics of Underdevelopment* | GB97 |
| Ashton, T. S. | *The Industrial Revolution* | GB109 |
| Austin, J. L. | *How To Do Things with Words* | GB132 |
| | *Sense and Sensibilia* | GB108 |
| Barker, Ernest, ed. & tr. | *The Politics of Aristotle* | GB69 |
| ed. | *Social Contract:* | |
| | *Essays by Locke, Hume, Rousseau* | GB68 |
| Bate, Walter Jackson | *The Achievement of Samuel Johnson* | GB53 |
| Berlin, Isaiah | *Karl Marx: His Life and Environment* | GB25 |
| Bogard and Oliver, eds. | *Modern Drama* | GB138 |
| Bowle, John | *Politics and Opinion in the 19th Century* | GB119 |
| Bowra, C. M. | *Ancient Greek Literature* | GB30 |
| | *The Romantic Imagination* | GB54 |
| Bridenbaugh, Carl and Jessica | *Rebels and Gentlemen:* | |
| | *Philadelphia in the Age* | |
| | *of Franklin* | GB141 |
| Brower, Reuben A. | *The Fields of Light* | GB87 |
| Bruun, Geoffrey | *Nineteenth Century European Civilization* | GB36 |
| Bush, Douglas | *English Poetry* | GB93 |
| Clark, George | *Early Modern Europe* | GB37 |
| | *The Seventeenth Century* | GB47 |
| Clifford, James L. | *Biography as an Art* | GB70 |
| ed. | *Eighteenth-Century English Literature* | GB23 |
| Cochrane, Charles Norris | *Christianity and Classical Culture* | GB7 |
| Collingwood, R. G. | *The Idea of History* | GB1 |
| | *The Idea of Nature* | GB31 |
| | *The Principles of Art* | GB11 |
| Cragg, Kenneth | *The Call of the Minaret* | GB122 |
| Craig, Gordon A. | *The Politics of the Prussian Army, 1640-1945* | GB118 |
| Cruickshank, John | *Albert Camus and the Literature of Revolt* | GB43 |
| Davis, Herbert | *Jonathan Swift: Essays on His Satire* | |
| | *and Other Studies* | GB106 |
| Dean, Leonard, ed. | *Shakespeare* | GB46 |
| Dixon, W. MacNeile | *The Human Situation* | GB12 |
| Ellmann, Richard | *The Identity of Yeats* | GB126 |
| Feidelson and Brodtkorb, eds. | *Interpretation of American Literature* | GB26 |
| Frankel, Joseph | *International Relations* | GB117 |
| Gerould, Gordon Hall | *The Ballad of Tradition* | GB8 |
| Gerth, H. H., and Mills, C. Wright, eds. & trs. | *From Max Weber:* | |
| | *Essays in Sociology* | GB13 |
| Gibb, H. A. R. | *Mohammedanism* | GB90 |
| Gilby, Thomas, ed. & tr. | *St. Thomas Aquinas: Philosophical Texts* | GB29 |

| | | |
|---|---|---|
| Grierson, Herbert, ed. | *Metaphysical Lyrics and Poems of the Seventeenth Century* | GB19 |
| Halsband, Robert | *The Life of Lady Mary Wortley Montagu* | GB44 |
| Hare, R. M. | *Freedom and Reason* | GB134 |
| | *The Language of Morals* | GB111 |
| Heiler, Friedrich | *Prayer,* translated by Samuel McComb | GB16 |
| Heimann, Eduard | *History of Economic Doctrines* | GB123 |
| Highet, Gilbert | *The Classical Tradition* | GB5 |
| | *Juvenal the Satirist* | GB48 |
| Hobhouse, L. T. | *Liberalism* | GB120 |
| Hoffman, Daniel | *Form and Fable in American Fiction* | GB137 |
| Kaplan, Abraham | *American Ethics and Public Policy* | GB99 |
| Kaufmann, R. J., ed. | *Elizabethan Drama* | GB63 |
| Keast, William R., ed. | *Seventeenth-Century English Poetry* | GB89 |
| Kennedy, Charles, ed. & tr. | *Early English Christian Poetry* | GB94 |
| Kerr, C., Dunlop, J. T., Harbison, F. H., & Myers, C. A. *Industrialism and Industrial Man* | | GB107 |
| Kitto, H. D. F., tr. | *Sophocles: Three Tragedies: Antigone; Oedipus the King; Electra* | GB114 |
| Kline, Morris | *Mathematics in Western Culture* | GB128 |
| Koch, Adrienne | *Jefferson and Madison: The Great Collaboration* | GB110 |
| Knox, Ronald A. | *Enthusiasm* | GB59 |
| Langer, Susanne K., ed. | *Reflections on Art* | GB60 |
| Lewis, C. S. | *The Allegory of Love* | GB17 |
| | *A Preface to Paradise Lost* | GB57 |
| Lindsay, A. D. | *The Modern Democratic State* | GB86 |
| Litz, A. Walton | *The Art of James Joyce* | GB121 |
| ed. | *Modern American Fiction* | GB100 |
| Lowrie, Walter, tr. | *Kierkegaard: Christian Discourses* | GB49 |
| Livingstone, Richard, ed. & tr. | *Thucydides: The History of the Peloponnesian War* | GB33 |
| MacNeice, Louis, tr. | *Goethe's Faust* | GB45 |
| Malinowski, Bronislaw | *A Scientific Theory of Culture* | GB40 |
| Matthiessen, F. O. | *The Achievement of T. S. Eliot* | GB22 |
| | *Henry James. The Major Phase* | GB103 |
| Matthiessen, F. O., and Murdock, Kenneth B., eds. | *The Notebooks of Henry James* | GB61 |
| Mills, C. Wright | *The Power Elite* | GB20 |
| | *White Collar* | GB3 |
| Montagu, Ashley, ed. | *Culture and the Evolution of Man* | GB88 |
| Morison, Samuel Eliot | *Sources and Documents Illustrating the American Revolution, 1764-1788, and the Formation of the Federal Constitution* | GB135 |
| Moss, H. St. L. B. | *The Birth of the Middle Ages, 395-814* | GB130 |
| Muller, Herbert J. | *The Uses of the Past* | GB9 |
| Mure, G. R. G. | *Aristotle* | GB113 |

| Murray, Gilbert | *The Rise of the Greek Epic* | GB41 |
| Nicholas, H. G. | *The United Nations as a Political Institution* | GB105 |
| Nicolson, Harold | *Diplomacy* | GB115 |
| Nisbet, Robert A. | *Community and Power* | GB91 |
| Otto, Rudolf | *The Idea of the Holy* | GB14 |
| Peterson, Merrill D. | *The Jefferson Image in the American Mind* | GB71 |
| Price, Don K. | *Government and Science* | GB72 |
| Radhakrishnan, S. | *Eastern Religions and Western Thought* | GB27 |
| Richards, I. A. | *The Philosophy of Rhetoric* | GB131 |
| Roberts, David E. | *Existentialism and Religious Belief,* edited by Roger Hazelton | GB28 |
| Rosenthal, M. L. | *The Modern Poets: A Critical Introduction* | GB139 |
| Rostovtzeff, M. | *Greece* | GB98 |
| | *Rome* | GB42 |
| Russell, Bertrand | *The Problems of Philosophy* | GB21 |
| | *Religion and Science* | GB50 |
| Schelling, Thomas C. | *The Strategy of Conflict* | GB101 |
| Schorer, Mark, ed. | *Modern British Fiction* | GB64 |
| Schumpeter, Joseph A. | *Ten Great Economists: From Marx to Keynes* | GB140 |
| | *The Theory of Economic Development,* translated by Redvers Opie | GB55 |
| Sesonske, Alexander | *Value and Obligation: The Foundations of an Empiricist Ethical Theory* | GB125 |
| Shapiro, Harry L., ed. | *Man, Culture, and Society* | GB32 |
| Shaw, T. E., tr. | *The Odyssey of Homer* | GB2 |
| Sinclair, John D., ed.& tr. | *Dante's Inferno* | GB65 |
| | *Dante's Purgatorio* | GB66 |
| | *Dante's Paradiso* | GB67 |
| Slonim, Marc | *The Epic of Russian Literature:* *From Its Origins through Tolstoy* | GB127 |
| | *From Chekhov to the Revolution* | GB92 |
| Tarski, Alfred | *Introduction to Logic and to the Methodology of Deductive Sciences* | GB133 |
| Thomson, David | *World History: 1914-1961* | GB116 |
| Thomson, George | *The Atom* | GB95 |
| Tillich, Paul | *Love, Power and Justice* | GB38 |
| | *Theology of Culture* | GB124 |
| Toynbee, Arnold J. | *A Study of History, Volume 1* | GB74 |
| | *A Study of History, Volume 2* | GB75 |
| | *A Study of History, Volume 3* | GB76 |
| | *A Study of History, Volume 4* | GB77 |
| | *A Study of History, Volume 5* | GB78 |
| | *A Study of History, Volume 6* | GB79 |
| | *A Study of History, Volume 7A* | GB80 |
| | *A Study of History, Volume 7B* | GB81 |
| | *A Study of History, Volume 8* | GB82 |

|  | A Study of History, Volume 9 | GB83 |
|  | A Study of History, Volume 10 | GB84 |
|  | A Study of History, Volume 12 | GB85 |
| ille, A. S. | English Men and Manners in the Eighteenth Century | GB10 |
| Wagenknecht, Edward, ed. | Chaucer | GB24 |
| Ward, John William | Andrew Jackson: Symbol for an Age | GB73 |
| Wedgwood, C. V. | Seventeenth-Century English Literature | GB51 |
| Wheare, K. C. | Federal Government | GB112 |
|  | Legislatures | GB104 |
| Whitehead, Alfred North | An Introduction to Mathematics | GB18 |
| Wilson, Edmund | The Triple Thinkers | GB96 |
|  | The Wound and the Bow: Seven Studies in Literature | GB136 |
| Woodward, C. Vann | Tom Watson: Agrarian Rebel | GB102 |
|  | The Strange Career of Jim Crow | GB6 |
| Wright, Austin, ed. | Victorian Literature | GB52 |
| Young, G. M. | Victorian England: Portrait of an Age | GB129 |
| Young, J. Z. | Doubt and Certainty in Science | GB34 |
| Zaehner, R. C. | Mysticism Sacred and Profane | GB56 |
| Zimmern, Alfred | The Greek Commonwealth | GB62 |

## HESPERIDES BOOKS

| Clifford, James | Young Sam Johnson | HS5 |
| Einstein, Alfred | Mozart: His Character, His Work | HS8 |
| Falls, Cyril | The Art of War from the Age of Napoleon to the Present Day | HS3 |
| Ferguson, George | Signs and Symbols in Christian Art | HS1 |
| Fry, Christopher | Three Plays: The Firstborn; Thor, with Angels; A Sleep of Prisoners | HS4 |
| Ibsen, Henrik | An Enemy of the People; The Wild Duck; Rosmersholm | HS2 |
| Tolstoy, Leo | What is Art? and Essays on Art | HS6 |